C000281348

Sepu

In the name of God, most Gracious, most Merciful

Building Muslim Families
Challenges and Expectations

Muhammad Abdul Bari

Ta-Ha Publishers Ltd.
1 Wynne Road,
London SW9 0BB
UK

Copyright © Muhammad Abdul Bari

Published Jumada al-Ula 1423/August 2002 by:
Ta-Ha Publishers Ltd.
1 Wynne Road
London SW9 0BB
Website: http://www.taha.co.uk
Email: sales@taha.co.uk

All rights reserved. No part of this publication may be reproduced, stored in any retrieval system, or transmitted in any form or by any means, electronic or otherwise, without written permission of the publishers.

By: Muhammad Abdul Bari
General Editor: Afsar Siddiqui
Edited by: Abdassamad Clarke

British Library Cataloguing in Publication Data
Abdul Bari, Muhammad
Building Muslim Families: Challenges and Expectations
I. Title

ISBN 1 84200 041 1

Typeset by: Bookwright
Website: http://www.bogvaerker.dk/Bookwright
Email: bookwright@bogvaerker.dk

Printed and bound by: Deluxe Printers, London.
NW10 7NR Tel. 020 8965 1771
Email: de-luxe@talk21.com

Contents

Foreword

It is indeed gratifying to note the appearance of Dr. M. A. Bari's *Building Muslim Families: Challenges and Expectations*, which is of immense value and relevance for the Muslim community.

In Islam marriage is the cornerstone of family life. Accordingly, Islam treats marriage as a sacred tie and an important step contributing to a better, purer and happier life. Marriage is recognised as the main means, sanctioned by Allah, for having children as part of perpetuating the human race. Needless to emphasise that the institution of the family is the cradle of civilisation. The love, care, and sacrifice which prompt parents, especially mothers, to look after and bring up their children are innate in human nature and represent Allah's blessing upon mankind. The same holds true for the parental affection and concern for children. A family setting therefore works wonders for children. They grow up as valued individuals from their childhood. Since family serves as the best training ground, children imbibe many values, particularly of respecting others and growing up with self-esteem. Regrettably, these invaluable institutions of marriage and family have been under tremendous pressure in modern society. Its consequences have already been appalling. The rampant social degeneration may be traced back to the undermining of these life-enriching institutions.

Dr. M. A. Bari, a competent educator by profession and a committed parenting-skills facilitator has written this highly useful book in the Islamic perspective. As a result of his long association with youth and community work he has gained many insights into the strengths and weaknesses of Muslim community life in the West. In the present work he has discussed the concept of marriage and family from a broader Islamic viewpoint and demonstrated the pitfalls of the modern Western lifestyle. His work is rooted firmly in the primary sources – the Qur'an and the Sunnah. In addition, he has drawn upon recent writings on the subject. He has therefore done a commendable job in spelling out a road map for Muslims in order to develop a healthy family life.

I am sure this work would go a long way in helping Muslims in the West to gain a better understanding of their role and responsibilities in marital and family life. This work is destined to be helpful in building a blessed Muslim family life. It is meant for all mankind, yearning to enjoy a happy, peaceful life. May Allah accept this work and reward those committed to the regeneration of our community.

Rabi' al-Awwal 1423 AH   Dr. Manazir Ahsan

June 2002 CE   Director General

                                                          The Islamic Foundation,

                                                          Leicester, UK

Acknowledgements

This book is the outcome of my long involvement with youth and community work in Britain. Many people, including the very young and old, have contributed to the ideas contained in it. They all deserve my sincere thanks. Like my other book, *The Greatest Gift: A Guide to Parenting from an Islamic Perspective*, the decision to write it was taken when I was running the 'Islamic Perspective of Parenting' course with an Internet-based virtual organisation, 'Witness Pioneer' in 2000. Since then it has been running almost every year. I am indebted to them for giving me the opportunity.

I express my deep appreciation for the contribution of my wife, Sayeda, for her understanding, support and contribution in writing the book. In spite of the pressure of life, her excellent family management and sense of humour continually encouraged me to sit at the computer. I am grateful to our four children, Rima, Raiyan, Labib and Adib for their enthusiasm during the process of writing. May Allah reward all of them with the best of rewards.

I am grateful to Dr. Hasan Shaheed, Rumman Ahmed, Ruqaiyyah Waris Maqsood and Dr. Jameel Qureshi for their valuable comments on the first draft. I am also indebted to a number of Ulama of the Islamic Forum Europe for helping me in finding references from the Qur'an and books of hadith.

May Allah shower His blessings on all of them.

Rabi' al-Awwal 1423 AH   Muhammad Abdul Bari
June 2002 CE

1

Introduction

With the increasing complexity of modern life Muslim families face many challenges. For Muslims living in the West keeping the family unit intact and raising children in Islam are becoming daunting prospects. Although there are exemplary features in the Muslim community regarding their family bonding and child rearing, unfortunately many Muslims do not seem well-equipped to withstand the storm of secular and materialistic ideas regarding man-woman relationships, marriage, family and other aspects of life. After the turbulent periods of the Renaissance and Reformation the modern West has become an amoral and permissive society. They are giving up many age-old religious and cultural values once based on Judaeo-Christian tradition. Now western societies are fast adapting to an ethos and culture that, in the past, were inimical to those teachings. Given their economic and media supremacy in the world, these values and this outlook on life are influencing the rest of the world. They are now being treated as the bastions of so-called modernity and progress and promoted globally with proselytising force.

On the other hand, present day Muslims are simply struggling to cope in the midst of this transformation of values. Many of them live in the past and find pleasure in roving through their lost glories of intellectual discourse and creative thinking. While 'traditionalists' tend to put their heads in the sand in order to escape from the future, 'secularists' want to ditch much of Islamic value at the altar of 'modernism'. Some are imprisoned in the mindset of the colonial legacy. Muslims are at a historical juncture. The post-September 11th world has brought new challenges and opportunities for us.

We know for sure that, over past centuries, things have gone terribly wrong for Muslims in many directions, including our family life. The immense pull of Jahiliyah, and the general ignorance, complacency and indifference among the Muslim masses are disturbing. Family breakdown and other social ills that have gripped Western society are there to engulf others, including Muslims. Unless addressed openly and robustly, this could bring psychological alienation in our children leading to social disaffection and spiritual emptiness. This may already be happening and may lead to a crisis for the Muslim community in the West.

The encouraging thing is that there is now a positive realisation in many quarters of the Muslim community of the need to work vigorously to build our future. It depends on how Muslims can best stand up to the challenges of modern materialistic life and address the issue of fortifying families to anchor their children in the positive ethos of Islam. If Muslims want to safeguard their Islamic identity, build their families and communities and work for the common good of humanity in the West, building families and raising children in Islam should be brought to the forefront of our agenda. Conscientious members of the Muslim community should join hands with the positive forces in the wider society to start a broader pro-family movement. Already this is gaining momentum in many Western countries.

The purpose of this book is, first, to raise awareness among Muslims about the ever-increasing importance of marriage as the only acceptable human relationship for sexual fulfilment and human continuity. It discusses different aspects of marriage, how and when it should be done and important issues, e.g., marital breakdown, divorce procedures, forced marriage, polygamy, etc.

Secondly, it discusses the family as a historic institution, the features and purposes of Muslim families, the rights and responsibilities of family members, and important issues related to the family, e.g., extended families, domestic violence, fostering, etc. The modern threat to the family and family values, the basic ingredients needed to make a blessed family, the ethos and principles of Muslim families, and the impediments that can cause family disharmony – all these have also been tackled briefly.

Family is the cradle of human civilisation. It is the centre for nurturing human beings, the emissaries of Allah on earth, preparing them to take on the generational task of sustaining stable societies. Family is the first nursery, and the school and university that produce a nation and civilisation. Although formal schools, community and governance play their vital role in nation building, they will surely fail if families fail in their job. A happy family environment is the best thing parents can give their children. Any parent who feels passionately about raising children properly should care first about building a sound family.

The book is written for ordinary Muslims who have a sense of urgency for their community's future and who want to do something about it. Human life is complex and as such there could be many approaches to addressing an issue, depending on cultural or other factors. Unless specified in the Shariah, any opinion in the book should be taken in that light and should not be taken as judgmental. The book is an educational and social one. Although broad Islamic principles are highlighted, it is not meant to be a book of Fiqh. I have followed the broad Islamic principle that anything not forbidden in Islam is generally acceptable. This book is an attempt to regenerate Muslim community in the West. I rely on the forgiveness of Allah for my shortcomings and pray that He accept this humble work.

NOTES

Translations of Qur'anic verses are based upon *The Meaning of the Glorious Koran* by Mohammed Marmaduke Pickthall and *The Noble Qur'an* by Abdalhaqq and Aisha Bewley.

It is established practice among Muslims to mention the supplication 鑗 – peace and blessing be upon him – after the Prophet Muhammad's name and this will be the practice here. Similarly, in the same manner, other prophets' names are followed by عليه السلام – peace be upon him – and companions' of the Prophet Muhammad 鑗 names are followed by رضي radiy'Allahu anhu/anha – may Allah be pleased be with him/her.

This book is written primarily for Muslims in the West. However, most examples are taken from Britain and, specifically, from the South Asian Muslim community. This should not, I think, jeopardise the common appeal of the book and I hope any reader can benefit from this. I am aware that the nature of this book may lead non-Muslim readers to erroneous view as to how Muslims perceive the West. The attempt to criticise the modern West has been done within a context and as objectively as possible. The 'East' and the Muslim world as it is at present has been criticised in the same manner. The purpose is to put forward the best of the two situations. I apologise if I have failed in maintaining objectivity.

1. The Institution of Marriage

Executive Summary – Part One

- THROUGHOUT HUMAN HISTORY, marriage has been the basis of family life. Premarital or extramarital sex is haram (forbidden) in Islam. Marriage is a social contract and a lifelong commitment.

- Marriage in Islam is sometimes an arranged one, but even then men and women should know each other as much as possible within the norms of Islam before marriage. Islam has put a boundary on mixing between the opposite sexes. The present concepts of 'boyfriend' and 'girlfriend' and experiencing a physical relationship before marriage are unacceptable. In Islamic marriage, the consent and choice of the man and woman are paramount. Generally, families from both sides but particularly from the side of the bride are involved. The marriage contract is a simple occasion in the presence of witnesses, with some prescribed requirements of *Shari'ah*.

- Early marriage is generally better, especially in permissive societies. One should not wait for an 'ideal time' to start a married life. However, a minimum level of economic solvency of the man and of the emotional and intellectual maturity of the couple are important. In choosing a marriage partner taqwa – awareness of Allah leading to avoiding acts of disobedience and embodiment of acts of obedience – should be given top priority, then there arises the need to look for areas of compatibility between them. Husbands and wives should recognise positive features in each other and overlook or forgive weaknesses.

- Marriage is better between Muslim men and women, but, Muslim men are permitted to marry chaste women of the Jews and Christians (*Ahl al-Kitab*, People of the Book), but not vice-versa. Polygamy is a recommended Sunnah on certain conditions. Forced marriage is prohibited.

- If for genuine reasons a marriage fails, there is room for divorce in Islam. However, it is the worst of all *halal* acts. Close relations are encouraged by *Shari'ah* to play their role in keeping the couple together. When a husband divorces his wife it is called *talaq* and when a wife gets a divorce from her husband it is *khul'*.

- With 'premarital sex' and 'living together' becoming common, marriage runs the risk of losing its importance in the modern West. Apart from giving rise to sexually transmitted diseases (STD), these social habits cause domestic violence, family breakdown, one-parent families and the resulting social disintegration.

- Children in marriage need to be looked after properly as gifts of Allah and raised in Islam so that they grow up to be responsible human beings. Whether born within the family or fostered, children have the right to good parenting.

1. THE SIGNIFICANCE OF MARRIAGE IN ISLAM

And of His signs is this: He created spouses for you of your own kind so that you might find tranquillity in them. And He has placed affection and mercy between you. (Qur'an 30: 21)

Allah has created everything in pairs and blessed them with physical and emotional attraction between the opposite sexes.

And We have created you in pairs. (Qur'an 78:8)

Marriage is part of my Sunnah, whoever runs away from my path is not from among us. (*Sahih al-Bukhari*)

The attraction towards and sexual desire for the opposite sex develop during the transformation from childhood to adolescence. The Islamic way of life leads young people toward lawful marriage that satisfies sexual, emotional and social needs. In permissive societies, teenage romance, encouraged by commercial, social and peer pressure, ends up in illicit physical relationships, often between socially and psychologically immature boys and girls. The result is obviously disastrous. Occasional news of 'underage' children (as low as twelve!) becoming parents of unwanted children creates sensation and worry. As premarital sex is legally acceptable in the modern West, teenage pregnancies cost us a great deal socially and economically. Britain has the highest percentage of teenage pregnancy in Europe. Even the heightened advertisement for 'safer sex', with condoms as the panacea, is failing to halt the rise of this social burden. This 'condom culture' is destroying the fabric of the society. As religious and spiritual values are looked down upon or sidelined, marriage as a social institution loses importance

The nature of teenage life is to explore new things and embark upon adventurous pursuits. Sex, being the most powerful passion in this age, can drive adolescents to lose focus in their lives and destroy the futures of many promising youngsters. Uncontrolled and irresponsible sexual relationships can ruin their careers and expectation of a normal life.

Marriage is a social contract between two human beings of opposite sex. It is also an institution that encompasses the joy of human relationship between a man and a woman. From the beginning of human history, men and women were bonded in marriage in order to have progeny, so that human continuity is never stopped. Marriage gave rise to families that formed tribes and races, societies and nations. This has continued so until recent decades, especially after the Second World War, since when marriage has been under threat from the fanatical proponents of liberalism and atheism.

Marriage is fundamental to the existence of human beings on earth. It is an institution that unites a man and a woman in mutual relationship and trust, for the purpose of establishing a family. Since ancient times, it has been a social practice and it reflects the character and customs of the society. Marriage is performed through a contractual procedure, normally based on revealed law. In some religions, e.g., Hinduism and until recently Christianity, the contract is inviolable. Marriage of influential people in history had influenced war and peace. All great religious traditions have considered marriage the basis of worldly peace.

Marriage provides solace, comfort and pleasure between two people. On the other hand, it teaches them compromise and sacrifice in order to live together under one roof. Throughout human history, marriage between a man and a woman provided the legal validation of children's social acceptance and legitimacy to inherit from their parents. Like other revealed religions, Islam places marriage as the only valid way to legitimate sex and have children, other than through the relationship with slave women*. The most important right of children is that they should be born within a stable home. They must not be the fruits of lust between a man and woman outside marriage. Adultery and fornication are two of the biggest wrong actions in all religions including Islam and, as such, their punishment is severe. As a result, marriage occupies a most important step in a Muslim's life. Allah has prescribed marriage as the main way for conjugal relationship and beginning a family (Qur'an 2:221, 5:5, 24:33). According to the Prophet Muhammad ﷺ, marriage is a 'half of the *deen*'.

When a slave of Allah marries, he completes half his deen, and he must have taqwa of Allah to complete the second half. (*Al-Bayhaqi*).

---

* Slave women are a part of the family and once they become mothers neither they nor their children can be sold. Sexual intercourse without responsibility for ensuing children and their mothers is absolutely not permitted.

Allah has blessed marriage with the following benefits:

- children
- it sublimates sexual passion
- peace of mind
- increase in divine service
- rewards for fulfilling one's duties to family

Sound family life teaches the importance of love, care, responsibility and affection. Inevitably, difficulties might arise in any human relationship that needs to be treated with care and compassion. The marriage bond encourages the development of faith, spirituality and social values among the partners. Obviously, the existence of children cements the bond between them. In Islam, husbands and wives are uniquely compared as 'garments to each other' (Qur'an 2:187). Marriage gives tranquillity of mind in the spouses (Qur'an 30:21).

Marriage is a lifelong commitment that definitely needs liveliness, love and affection between the couple for its long-term survival. Mutual love and affection, the *Sakinah* – tranquillity – that come after the wedding are long-lasting and can be eternal, even after death, if both husband and wife strive within the boundaries of Islam. The love and affection of the Prophet ﷺ for his wives, particularly Umm al-Mu'minin Sayyidatuna Khadijah and A'ishah, to mention two jewels of the Prophetic household, is a role model for all time to come. This is a reminder to those who think that married life is dull.

Marriage is for a divine purpose. In some societies, not long ago, marriage was encouraged to produce more children so that they become 'productive members of the society'. While in agricultural societies, this still remains so, marriage in developed countries is gradually becoming a burden. The Prophet Muhammad ﷺ has asked Muslims to marry on time and lead a balanced life on earth. He also advised Muslims to have children so that his *ummah* becomes large in number on the Day of Judgement. Celibacy, unless for some unavoidable reasons, is not encouraged in Islam. He said ﷺ:

Marriage is from my Sunnah. Marry women who are beloved and loving and bear children, because I shall be proud of my ummah on the Day of Judgement. (*Abu Dawud* and *an-Nasa'i*)

A group of three men came to the houses of the wives of the Prophet ☼ asking how he worshipped Allah, and they were informed about that. They considered their worship insufficient and said, "Where are we from the Prophet ☼ as his past and future wrong actions have been forgiven"? Then one of them said, "I will offer the prayer throughout the night forever." The other said, "I will fast throughout the year and will not break my fast." The third said, "I will keep away from women and not marry them ever." Allah's Messenger ☼ came to them and said, "Are you the same people who said so-and-so? By Allah, I am more submissive to Allah and more afraid of him; yet I fast and break my fast, I sleep and also marry women. So, he who doesn't follow my Sunnah is not from me (not one of my followers). (*Sahih al-Bukhari*)

Islam is opposed to selfishness and greed. Infanticide, abortion and avoiding or delaying having children just for fear of poverty is hateful in Islam. This is unbecoming of human dignity

Do not kill your children out of fear of being poor. We will provide for them and you. Killing them is a terrible mistake. (Qur'an 17:31)

2. ARRANGING MARRIAGE

In an Islamic marriage, the consent and choice of the man and woman is paramount. However, families from both sides can be involved. In this context, marriage in Islam is often broadly an arranged one. In Muslim culture, every relevant person in the family contributes to building a new family. The family and the society all have stakes in the success of a Muslim marriage. Parents, relatives and friends often help in their own ways to find marriage partners for their loved ones. The post-puberty boys and girls are themselves allowed to choose their life partners within the norms and decencies of Islam. However, Islam has a social code for the interaction between men and women. Dating, clubbing and 'free mixing' are considered unacceptable. Muslim men and women have been asked to follow the Qur'anic command of lowering their gaze when they encounter the opposite sex.

> Say to the believing men that they should lower their eyes and guard their private parts. That is purer for them. Allah is aware of what they do. Say to the believing women that they should lower their eyes and guard their private parts and not display their adornments, except for what normally shows ... (Qur'an 24:30,31).

Courtship for marriage is not allowed in Islam. Premarital 'boyfriend-girlfriend' relationships for fun and romance are alien to Muslim culture. Cohabitation or 'living together' is a grave wrong action in Islam. However, in a liberal social environment it is not unlikely that 'innocent love' or a natural liking may grow between two young Muslims while studying or working together. This is an issue many parents may want to sweep under the carpet. In cases like this, wise parents need to be open to their children and advise them how to remain within the boundaries of Islam. If, in this type of situation, parents realise that marriage is the only solution they should arrange it without any delay. Young Muslims should be reminded that men and women who are not closely related (*mahram*) should not meet each other in seclusion.

> Whenever a man sits with a woman in privacy, a third one always creeps in, and that is shaytan. (*At-Tirmidhi*)

Decent interaction for valid reasons between a man and woman in the presence of others is different from this. The purpose of this apparently 'strict' segregation of man and woman is to save them from the pitfalls in their character and from laxity of morals and conduct. Without adherence to the guidelines given by Allah, man and woman can embark on a path that may lead to sexual mayhem in the society. Unfortunately, this is what seems to be happening now.

A Simple Social Occasion

Marriage is a happy occasion and the contract is public so that relevant people from both the bride and the groom's sides can participate in the joy. The Prophet Muhammad ﷺ instructed Muslims to announce marriages publicly and arrange a feast according to their financial capacity. The marriage ceremony or *Nikah* is very simple and has some essential requirements[1], such as:

- the consent of bride and groom
- consent of the bride's guardian
- the presence of two Muslim witnesses
- agreement on the groom's *mahr* (dower) for the bride

Unfortunately, due to alien cultural influences, marriage in many Muslim communities has been marred by practices unacceptable in Islam. The simplicity prescribed by Islam is gradually being replaced by inessential social customs. Worse even, is the unfortunate financial bargaining by one or the other party in some Muslim communities. Instead of a serene and reflective atmosphere many marriage ceremonies are expensive extravaganza with unnecessary free-mixing and artificial pomp. The practice of asking for a higher dower, *mahr*, has become a major social disease in many Muslim societies. In some areas in South Asia the bridegroom's family demands huge cash or other 'presents' from the bride's family, which is absolutely against Islam since it is the groom who gives his bride a dowry. On the other hand, young men in some countries cannot marry at the appropriate age because of the inflated social prestige linked with the high *mahr* demanded by the woman's family, which they are unable to pay. In some societies, this leads to nonpayment or part-payment, and often to outright cheating of women. *Mahr* is the right of a woman – given by Allah – from her husband. Without it, marriage is unacceptable. The Prophet Muhammad ﷺ arranged marriage with an affordable *mahr*, in one case for some dates from one of his male companions who was very poor. Marriage is a serious affair that has no room for deception. Muslims who understand the meaning of marriage cannot think of this ploy, whatever the social pressure may be. Islam has prohibited such *mahr* as is beyond a bridegroom's capacity. Fortunately, with young Muslims coming back to Islam this practice is now diminishing.

Mahr: **A Muslim woman's right**   In a highly colourful wedding ceremony, where there were hundreds of guests in a big town hall, the imam gave a short emotional speech before the *nikah* and talked about the simplicity of Muslim marriage. During the wedding, announcement was made of the excessively high dower for the bride. Probably nobody noticed it, but a couple of non-Muslim guests, who were colleagues of the groom, were startled to hear the amount. They knew the groom could never pay this amount of money to his wife. One of them whispered to the other, "if the Muslim marriage is so simple, then how is our colleague going to pay his dower?" The other looked puzzled and said, "I have the same question". They could not hide their anxiety and asked one middle-aged Muslim near them. The man smiled at their ignorance and said, "Don't worry, it's just a formality. He will never pay it." A further surprise for the two gentlemen! They asked him, "But the imam categorically mentioned it as the bride's marital right. How can he avoid that?" The man giggled as if he was feeling pity on them. He then answered like an expert, "You know, the groom will never pay, because he will get it waived from the bride on the first night. It's our practice, I did the same thing in the first night of my marriage." The two gentlemen were astounded to hear this. While I was overhearing this conversation, a feeling of unease ran through my veins. Should I leave my seat and interrupt the so-called Muslim 'expert'? I decided not to at that moment, as this could prove disastrous.

Choosing a Marriage Partner

Marriage in Islam is by means of a proposal, and both parties give priority to taqwa, good character and compatibility. A couple having little in common, in terms of essential qualities, would find it difficult to hold together for long. The Prophet Muhammad ﷺ was a pragmatic leader, and on one occasion he advised Fatimah bint Qays, a woman companion, to marry Usamah ibn Zayd, the son of his freed slave and adopted son, instead of one of two other companions, e.g., Mu'awiyah and Abu Jahm, because of his concern for their compatibility. (Sahih Muslim). Truthful, honest and believing men and women look for similar qualities in their partners. On the other hand, partners with low qualities will naturally cling to each other

Table 2.1 Prominent features to look for in potential husbands and wives

Husband	Wife
• Understanding and commitment to Islam.	• Understanding and commitment to Islam.
• Honesty, integrity and reliability.	• Honesty, integrity and reliability.
• Social and life skills relevant to men.	• Social and life skills relevant to women.
• Sacrifice and ability to accommodate.	• Sacrifice and ability to accommodate.
• Education and professional expertise primarily to earn for the family.	• Education and professional expertise primarily to raise children in Islam.
• Family background.	• Family background.
• Strength of character as in the role of a provider and protector in the family.	• Loyalty to husband in goodness.
• Positive outlook, magnanimity and broad-mindedness.	• Liveliness.
• Ability to cope with anger, crisis and external pressure.	• Interest and skills in household chores.
• Competence and enthusiasm to lead a family in Islamic ethos.	• Feminine qualities, e.g., tenderness and care.
• Willingness to consult.	• Ability to cope with domestic pressure and the demands of children.
• Equity, impartiality and sense of justice.	
• Masculine features, e.g., toughness and stamina.	

Table 2.2 A few major questions to ask potential husbands and wives

Husband

- Is he medically sound?
- Does his family have any bad history?
- Does he understand women's rights in Islam and is he ready to accept those in his case?
- Is he stingy in financial affairs?
- Does he easily become angry and does he blame others for this?
- Does he have any bad habits, e.g., smoking?
- Is he macho or self-centred?

Wife

- Is she medically sound?
- Does her family have any bad history?
- Does she understand a husband's rights in Islam and is she ready to accept that in her case?
- What view does she have on having babies and rearing them?
- Is she an individualist or feminist?

Corrupt women are for corrupt men and corrupt men are for corrupt women, good women are for good men and good men are for good women. (Qur'an 24:26).

Choosing a marriage partner[2] is a challenging job. Marriage is about bonding two hearts and is thus dependent on Allah's blessings. For a successful marriage, both partners need to satisfy each other regarding the issues they feel important, no matter how trivial they seem to be. Family background, personality traits, habits, attitude and manners – all are important. Although no marriage can succeed without the spirit of compromise, the major issues need to be sorted before a match is finalised. Women probably need more assurance on some aspects of men, even though a Muslim society may have the support mechanism.

Islam does not adhere to the concept of unnatural social strata in marrying two Muslims. Human beings' identities as 'high caste' or 'low caste' is alien to Islam and that comes from the days of ignorance or the ancient caste systems in some communities. However, Islam looks for genuine 'compatibility' and 'wisdom'[3] for a social, intellectual, economic and educational match between two partners in marriage. Compatibility in age is also important. Although, on occasion, the Prophet Muhammad ﷺ encouraged a male companion to marry virgin girls, there should not be any stigma in marrying widows, because he himself married widows. He advised Muslims not to marry only for the sake of beauty, as desire for beauty often brings moral decline. He has also advised us not to marry only for the sake of wealth, as wealth often becomes the reason for disobedience to Allah. He asked Muslim men to look for *taqwa* in women so that children will get a proper Islamic upbringing. Beauty and wealth are extra blessings. According to traditions:

> A woman is married for four things: her wealth, her beauty, her lineage or her deen. Always choose a woman for her deen. (*Sahih al Bukhari, Muslim, Abu Dawud* and *an-Nasa'i*)

17

This world is all temporary conveniences, and the greatest joy in this life is a right-acting wife. (*Muslim*)

Marriage provides soothing comfort to the partners in life. Allah has given to women probably the greater share of mercy, love and compassion. Men, on the other hand, are bestowed with strong will and assertive and adventurous natures. For a man to succeed in marriage his intellectual maturity and accommodative quality are vitally important. Muslims, both men and women, are advised to supplicate for Allah's choice (*istikharah*) while choosing a marriage partner. "None fails who consults (others) and none regrets who seeks (the Creator's) choice" (*At-Tabarani*). Below is a list of some prominent features to look for and major questions to ask potential husbands and wives. One cannot expect all positive features in one's partner. On the other hand, one probably cannot get excellent answers to all questions from the other. Marriage is a compromise and people should reflect upon their own strengths and weaknesses in order to be realistic in life.

3. WHEN TO MARRY?

When should a Muslim marry? The answer is in the *Sunnah* of the Prophet. Islam prefers marriage at the right age, i.e., sooner after puberty, when a boy or girl becomes physically, emotionally and intellectually mature, and is fit to take up responsibility. Marriage involves social and economic responsibility. A man has to have a minimum of economic sustainability to maintain a family. Marriage is a joyful event and the earlier the better. The youthful couple can play with each other and with their children so as to enjoy the pleasure of life in a *halal* way. Children are the products of marriage. For lively engagement with the children, early marriage helps youthful parents to face the challenges of rearing young ones. Marriage is a conscious commitment to a life-partner for a future family role, and a serious job that affects the spouses, the children, and the community.

As regards minimum economic sustainability, one does not have to have the ideal preparation for starting a family. *Halal* income that can support the couple with dignity is the prerequisite. In spite of existing discrimination on the basis of ethnicity and faith, Western countries are still a better place for jobs and decent earnings, thanks to their economy and welfare arrangements. In this social condition, young Muslims, in general, probably have the opportunity to start families in their early twenties. However, they need to prepare themselves from their school life and explore the available opportunities for the best *halal* income. It is imperative they increase their professionalism and skills through education and hard work, so that they can live with dignity and become active partners in the society.

> The first thing of the human body to purify is the abdomen, so he who can eat nothing but good food (*halal* and lawfully earned) should do so… (*Sahih al-Bukhari*)

> The flesh that is nurtured with *haram* wealth cannot enter the Garden. The Fire is his abode. (*Musnad al-Bari*)

In Islam, earning is primarily the man's responsibility in the family. He is burdened with this job from the beginning of human creation. But seeking knowledge is compulsory for both men and women. Illiteracy and ignorance among women bring danger to the family. Muslim women in the past were pioneers in their contributions to the *ummah* in many areas of life. Women in other cultures, e.g., Florence Nightingale and Emily Pankhurst in the West, were pioneers in establishing the rights of women in their days. However, Islam has not required Muslim women to earn for the family, unless felt by both spouses for some good reasons, such as alleviating family hardship or contributing a special skill to the society. The wife has a right, according to *Shari'ah*, in the earnings of her husband. But the husband has no right over her earnings. Thus, it is also inappropriate for Muslim women to ignore their young children and go outside the home to earn without valid reason. This has a negative effect in the formative period of young children and at the same time puts extra pressure on them. As the children grow, they can take up careers in consultation with their husbands. In any case, rearing children in Islam and giving them quality time are important for both parents.

The 'right time' to get married is very much linked to a conscious understanding of Islam and *tawakkul* (reliance on Allah), not merely on good earnings. Young Muslims should not wait for an 'ideal time', as it will probably never come in anybody's life. Pakistani and Bangladeshi young people in Britain are still marrying in their early twenties[4]. Provided Islamic teaching is kept alive in the community, this practice will stand the test of time.

In the modern West where promiscuous relationships have become a trend and marriage is losing its significance, Muslim boys and girls should leave no stone unturned in preparing themselves for early marriage so that the allurements of the opposite sex cannot drive their passion into un-Islamic acts. Caliph Umar ؓ said, "Two things prevent marriage – inability and being a wrongdoer". Of course, the decision to marry is a big step for a young person, and conscientious parents should play an active role in encouraging their mature son or daughter to marry early. If for some genuine reason there is delay in marrying, young men and women should follow the Prophet's *Sunnah* of fasting.

> The Prophet ﷺ said, "O young men! whoever among you is able to marry, should marry and whoever is not able should fast regularly, as this will be a shield for him." (*Sahih al-Bukhari* and *Muslim*)

4. IMPORTANT ISSUES IN MARRIAGE

Marrying a Non-Muslim

Allah permits Muslim men to marry women from *Ahl al-Kitab* (People of the Book, i.e., Jews and Christians). As a result, some Muslim men settling in the West take advantage by marrying Christian or Jewish women who have little adherence to their own religions. What is the success rate of these marriages? How are the children raised, in terms of their religion and culture, in these dual-faith families? To be fair, the situation is generally disappointing. Apart from some exceptions, where the Muslim men have strong roots in Islam, many of these marriages either end in mutual recrimination or create situations where the children become the casualties. They grow up with torn identities and confusion in their lives. Young Muslim men should keep the following Qur'anic verse in mind, when marrying a woman from the People of the Book.

> Made lawful to you on this day are … (in marriage) chaste women from the believers and chaste women from those who were given the Scripture before you. (Qur'an 5:5)

Muslims always look for long-term human benefit. Children are assets for any human society. That is why some Muslim scholars have advised that such marriages should only be practised in Muslim lands where the environment for rearing children in Islam is positive. Caliph Umar 🕮 discouraged believing men from marrying outside Islam in his period, fearing that Muslim men might leave Muslim women unmarried.

Muslim women are prohibited from marrying non-Muslim men under any circumstances, a prohibition followed by Muslims over the last fourteen hundred years. In recent times, due to the heavy secular influences in some Muslim families, women are seen marrying non-Muslim men. However small the number may be, this sad state of affairs is the sign of a disease. A recent sensational love affair between a Bahraini princess and a non-Muslim US Marine soldier highlighted the degeneration within the upper echelons of some Muslim societies. A young Muslim woman raised in Islam would have attempted to invite the man to Islam before marriage. Islam should take precedence over any worldly desire.

Polygamy

Polygamy is a misunderstood topic that evokes excited debate in the West. The media love to distort the image of Islam on this. Islam does allow polygamy, albeit for reasons. However, throughout the *ummah* today, monogamy is more common and polygamy is an exception. Why and when Muslim men are allowed to practise polygamy is a major topic.

Polygamy was a normal practice among Semitic and other peoples throughout history and many people around the world do still practise it for various reasons. In Islam polygamy is quite specific and is for men only. It is true that women find it psychologically difficult to 'share' their husbands and this also creates some family tension. It is also true that men find it difficult to maintain 'justice' among wives. But there are situations when polygamy is the only recourse that brings welfare to society. The Qur'an (Chapter 4, Verse 3) has mentioned the conditions when a man can enter into polygamy and limited the number to four. Islam is for justice to men and women. It is true that some Muslim men from some culture abuse this system for their own desire or self-interest for which women suffer. However, anyone fearing Allah will not play with Islam.

Polygamy in Islam ensures that men give women their rights as wives. Its permissibility saves the society from men having numerous mistresses without marital rights. Men and women in most cases just become sex-partners, with women often suffering domestic violence. Allah has set four as the limit at any one time so that marriage does not become a farce. This is the just decision by the Creator of both men and women. For biological, psychological and social reasons, Islam has prohibited polyandry.

Forced Marriage

Forced marriage has recently got a lot of media attention in Britain because of the allegation that some parents take their girls to their countries of origin and forcibly give them in marriage to their kin. There are also reports that girls are 'tricked' to marry someone, sometimes double their age, for reasons of economics or immigration. This happens because the family environment is such that girls cannot openly oppose it. As a result, what should be the most momentous event in a young woman's life ends up in misery. This cruel and unjust practice is found in some communities in South Asia. Unfortunately, some Muslims are also engrossed in this *Jahiliyyah*. Two Muslim Peers in the British Parliament, Lord Ahmed and Baroness Uddin, led a working group on Forced Marriage which, later on, published a report, titled "A Choice by Right". This highlighted the plight of women in forced marriage.

Surely, like all parents, Muslims love their children and do not want to see them unhappy in their marital lives The reasons that some of them do not leave any choice for their daughters and, in some cases, sons, lie in their strong misconceived sense of duty and faulty interpretation of family honour. But the damage done because of this is far-reaching, particularly in the West. Naturally, for any unhappy marriage of this sort parents get the blame. But the wider implications are many. In addition to media bashing of Islam, young Muslim girls undergo distress and some even rebel against what they consider Islam's 'oppression' of women by running away from home. A small number of these women go as far as joining Islam-bashing groups to take 'revenge'. The increase in the number of disenchanted Muslim girls in Western countries, unheard of in the past, is a cause for concern.

Islam has nothing to do with forced marriage. The Prophet of Islam ﷺ annulled at least one marriage which was done forcibly and which the woman did not accept.

If a man gives his daughter in marriage in spite of her disagreement, such a marriage is invalid. (*Sahih al-Bukhari*)

A young woman called Khansa bint Khidam once came to the Prophet ﷺ complaining that her father wished to force her to marry her cousin. The Prophet ﷺ told her that she had the right to reject her father's choice. But Khansa replied, "I accept my father's choice, but I wished to let the people know that our guardians cannot force us in marriage." (*Ahmad, Ibn Majah* and *an-Nasa'i*)

However, Islamic marriage has some discipline. In order for a marriage to be valid a Muslim girl needs the approval of her guardian, e.g., father, uncle, brother or others approved by *Shari'ah*. The Prophet Muhammad ﷺ said, "A woman's marriage without the consent of her guardian is void". (*Ahmad*)

5. MARITAL BREAKDOWN

Unwanted though this result may, marriage can also go wrong and fail. The 'empty-shell' marriage can occur due because of many reasons, such as:

- loss of physical and emotional love and warmth between husband and wife
- unrealistic expectations from each other
- rudeness and abuse from husband or wife
- mistrust between them
- unwanted intrusions of family members
- infertility and impotence
- infidelity
- insanity

In modern societies the secularism-driven concept of gender roles can be a major factor in marital breakdown. As man's leadership in the family is tested after marriage, young Muslim men have extra burdens in shouldering their responsibilities to Allah. Many young Muslim men brought up in the West lack the necessary maturity, tolerance and intellectual strength, and fail in their roles as husbands. In the same way young Muslim women have to have the strength to bring their egoism under control, so that they do not wreck the family by disobeying their husbands. Like any other human organisation, family members have complementary roles in order to make it work. There are rights and responsibilities in the family.

Whatever the reasons for marital problems, instead of living a hellish life in an unsuccessful marriage, Islam has allowed *Talaq* or *Khul* – two types of divorce, one for men and the other for women – on genuine grounds. Allah has revealed a whole chapter on the subject in the Qur'an, i.e., Surat at-Talaq. However, divorce is the most disliked of those things that are acceptable in Islam.

Prophet Muhammad ﷺ said, "Of all things permitted by law, divorce is the most disliked by Allah." (*Sunan Abu Dawud*).

Islam advocates *Sabr* – steadfastness – and as such divorce should not be done in haste. As it is painful, it needs a lot of reflection and mature consideration. Both partners should have enough time and space to think objectively about its implications. Could they reconcile on their own? What sorts of sacrifices are needed to mend their differences? How much can a member of the family or someone closer help in this? One has to weigh up all the positive and negative factors in taking this serious decision. If every sensible effort fails and divorce becomes inevitable this should be done amicably, before the relationship becomes too bitter. Islam has saved husbands and wives from the 'better dead than divorced' situation. Marriage is not life imprisonment.

Divorce is not a light thing. Misunderstandings about divorce have led Muslim men in some Muslim communities to frequently divorce wives or, on the contrary, refuse to grant divorce. Some of them keep their wives hanging in a kind of suspension. This is deplored in Islam. This unfortunate male attitude creates simmering discontent among Muslim women in some cultures. Once marriage comes to a breaking point, amicable divorce is the only solution. Sadly, there is still some social stigma attached to the status of divorced women that needs to be removed. Divorced women have the same right to remarry as divorced men.

Muslim divorce is relatively less complicated (Qur'an 2:226-237). Islamic procedures are to be followed in earnest[6] if the couple want to please Allah. *Talaq* occurs when a man decides to divorce his wife according to the appropriate guidelines. When a woman wants divorce from her husband she has to undergo a process called *Khul'*. The Islamic method of divorce allows both spouses to think ahead before the final separation.

The uniqueness of the marriage and divorce procedures has

kept divorce in Muslim societies to a minimum, unlike in the developed countries where the rate of divorce has been on the rise for decades. It is sad that a couple who declared 'their marriage made in heaven' or that 'theirs was an unbreakable bond' cannot continue as husband and wife for even one year. Ironically, some separated couples in the West find pleasure in 'living together' after their legal separation.

As a result of social changes brought about by the Reformation and the Industrial Revolution and with the advent of other materialistic ideologies the institution of marriage[7] has been transformed in Western societies in recent centuries. Arranged marriage was a common practice in the mediaeval West. It then moved to the phase of 'romantic' marriage, based on 'dating' or 'steady dating' leading to 'courtship'. Now marriage is losing prominence, giving rise to cohabitation with little lifetime commitment to one another. The changed economic status of women, liberalisation of divorce laws, legalisation of abortion, increased availability of contraceptives, social acceptance of so-called 'love children' – are all contributing to the widespread breakdown of marriage.

As marriage in the West is losing importance, the divorce rate is increasing. Almost every country in the Western world is now observing a rapid reduction in marriage as an enduring man-woman relationship. In Britain, the marriage rate has plummeted and the divorce rate increased significantly in three decades (1971 to 1999).[8] The trend is similar in the developing countries of the West.[9] The continuous rise in the rate of young people cohabiting without marriage is taking its toll on the social structure. Nowadays, even the Church seems to be accommodating this unwedded man-woman relationship.

There is social pressure on young people to conform to the nerve-wracking exercise of picking their 'boyfriends' or 'girlfriends' with a view to having a 'good time' or 'fun' with the opposite sex. Here the 'boy meets girl' experience gives rise to premarital sex, resulting in unwanted pregnancy in many cases, even after continuous bombardment with the 'safe sex' message. Women suffer most in this sexual mayhem. As men often run away from their responsibilities, women struggle as 'lone parents', some of them in their early teens. The result is emotional trauma, career loss and unfortunate social stigma. For many, antipathy towards deceitful and selfish male partners creates a general aversion towards men. 'Women prefer pets compared to partners', a survey for Britain's Pfizer Animal Health found in May 2000 that 54% of women with a pet considered it their best friend. A psychologist, June Nicholas, commented on this issue that pets give their owners emotional support.

Why is the modern West changing direction from its Judaeo-Christian orientation on marriage and divorce? The answer lies in its historical development. With the erosion of religious values and the rise of the egoistic concept of individual self-fulfilment and materialism, the institution of marriage is often considered 'bondage' to structured family life and a curtailment of personal freedom and space. When marriage is treated as the tool of patriarchal control over women, the family loses its spirit. The result is unhealthy for all in the community.

6. Marriage and Parenting

The natural fruit of marriage is the birth of children. Children are the products of physical love between a man and a woman. Those who fail to have children, sometimes opt to foster or adopt them. Such is the urge for parenthood that is embedded in human nature.

When adolescent boys and girls think about marriage they intend to embark upon an irreversible life journey, and are destined never to be the same again. Before marriage individuals can apparently lead their life according to their own plans, although other adults might have influences over them. They adopt lifestyles and habits of their own or influenced by their parents or some other people. Their maturity and responsibility remain limited. But, once they tie the knot with another human being, their life changes altogether. Human love between the spouses shifts the centre of their world. They have the same parents, siblings, friends and colleagues, but the new person takes over many of their priorities in life. With two families coming closer, new relatives come into the picture. Many rights and responsibilities are opened up inadvertently and they feel obliged to take care of them. The newlyweds initially find it hard to cope with all these demands, and they need support from people close to them.

The newlyweds need to spend some time exclusively with each other in order to come to grips with each other's strengths and weaknesses. The concept of the 'honeymoon' probably derives from this urgency to give the couple some time and space. For some time they may be at the height of their emotions and roam around in a world of idealism. However, they come down to reality and need to assess each other in order to clarify their positions on some of the hard realities of life so that they can reorient the focus of their life and formulate their planning regarding livelihoods, broader family matters, having children, etc.

Couples who can adapt quickly to the new realities bring order and balance in their life. They find their life challenging but enjoyable. Some may lose balance altogether and tend to undermine their responsibilities to parents and others in the heat of the love for their spouse. Muslim life should always have balance and justice. Duties toward a spouse do not remove or override duties toward others in the family, to community and the *ummah*. All of them are important in their own places. A balanced person has the ability to work out priorities in rights and in responsibilities to Allah and His creatures.

However, the most important aspect of a married life is the conscious choice to have children and to undertake their upbringing. Muslims never forget that the blessing of parenthood for a couple comes from Allah Who alone can create life. A right acting couple look for right acting children and in their sincere efforts to this goal they rely on Allah. No human being has any control over whether or not a new life will come in a family. The conception, growth and birth of a child is a mystery and nobody knows whether a baby will be physically and mentally complete or born with some handicap. The Prophet Muhammad ﷺ advised Muslims to remember Allah in supplication even in the ecstatic moment of physical union.

Thus, parenthood starts from the moment a man and woman start their married life. It is a massive job in itself that involves creative planning, dedication and sacrifice. Looking after vulnerable young creatures, giving them warmth and love, providing them with comfort and security, and raising them in Islam, is a full-time commitment. A couple seeking the pleasure of Allah and looking for a meaningful life should be emotionally prepared to bear all these burdens.

Parenthood is a historic journey that brings challenges and rewards in a married life. It can be the most pleasurable and worthwhile engagement in life. A couple's long-term plan is absolutely vital for the development of children's physical, intellectual, moral and spiritual life. Parenting becomes part of family life. Skills become necessary, particularly in the complex modern societies of the West. *'The hand that rocks the cradle rules the world'*. Nations that cater for proper nourishment and development of their children outperform others. Those who fail lose out.

NOTES

[1] *Raising Children in Islam*, Suhaib Hasan, pp18-22, Qur'an Society, London, 1998.

[2] *Bent Rib: A Journey through women's issue in Islam* by Huda-al-Khattab, p15, Ta-ha Publishers, London 1997.

[3] *The family Structure in Islam* by Hammudah Abd al-Ati, pp94-97, American Trust Publication, 1977.

[4] *Social Focus on Ethnic Minorities – A Publication of the Government Statistical Service, Crown Copyright, HMSO, 1996.*

[5] *Woman in Shari'ah* by Abdur Rahman I Doi, p92, Ta-Ha, London 1989.

[6] *Role of Muslim Woman in Society* by Afzalur Rahman, p153, Sirah Foundation London.

[7] *Sociology: Themes and Perspectives* by Haralambos and Holborn, pp370-377

[8] *National Statistics – Annual abstract of Statistics 2001 edition*, HMSO, UK, No137, p31, p40 and p42.

[9] *1998 Demographic Yearbook*, United Nations, New York, 2000.

2. Family: An Islamic Perspective

Executive Summary – Part Two

- FAMILY IS THE BEDROCK OF HUMAN CIVILISATION, in which men and women have complementary roles. Man is the leader in the context of the family, but has are rights and responsibilities. Children have the right to their physical, intellectual and spiritual nourishment. Working for children's Islamic development is more important than giving them food and good education.
- Muslim families are open families and often extended, unlike contemporary nuclear families of modern societies. A Muslim home provides a base for its members where right action is the norm and wrong action is minimised. The family is a centre of love and mercy. However, love for Allah and His Prophet ﷺ supersedes everything.
- Muslim families should have certain features to make them sources of inspiration for their members and others in the community. Through consultation and active participation of all family members, Muslims perform their divine responsibilities in this primordial human organisation.
- Fostered or adopted children or step-children should be treated the same as the couple's own children. No child in the family should have any restrictions placed on its growth.

31

- The family, as an institution, is now breaking down in the West and, as a result, family values are being eroded in the society. Broken- or one parent- families and gay families are now growing in numbers. This has dangerous implications for raising children. Muslims should be aware of these pitfalls so that they do not fall into them.

- Parents must know what happens in the wider society in order to raise their children with positive Islamic values. Openness and clarity are essential for creating a learning environment in the family. Family loyalty is vital to the members. Sacrifice from the parents enhances the family bond and creates an Islamic ethos for children.

7. THE FORTRESS FAMILY AND HUMAN CIVILISATION

O mankind! Be careful of your duty to your Lord Who has created you from a single self and from it created its mate and then disseminated many men and women from the two of them. Be careful of your duty toward Allah in Whose name you claim demands on one another, and toward the wombs (that bare you). Lo! Allah has been a Watcher over you. (Qur'an 4:1)

Family has always been the bedrock of human society. It gives mooring, anchor, stability and tranquillity to its members. It provides affection and emotional support to infants and young children. It gives roots to older children. It teaches them values and responsibility in the social context.

The family is a primary social group united through bonds of kinship or marriage. It provides its members with protection, companionship and security. The family has evolved since the beginning of human history and the multiplicity of families gave rise to clans, tribes and races. It has been the cradle of human civilisation since Adam and Hawa, our first father and mother, who cultivated the earth and who, as husband and wife, formed the human race.

As the first human family multiplied into multitudes over the millennia, families have maintained their original nature, with a clear division between male and female tasks, it being natural that when women gave birth and their duties looking after children grew onerous, the tasks outside the home of the men should grow more important. The physical and emotional features of men and women made this all the more natural. This has continued to be so in most societies. However, in modern technological countries, due to the needs of finance and industrial society, there are growing changes in their structures and in the roles of men and women in society. As the number of children born to a woman decreases, her role in the family and society is also changing dramatically. The concept of a nuclear family with two adults and some children is becoming the norm. Most often this dwindles even further to the lone mother struggling with her one or two children. With the rising demand for both men and women as workers in the financial-industrial complex and the compensatory individualism and self-centredness, people are becoming cut off from a wider family network, giving rise to loneliness, depression and stress. The advent of modern technological gadgets has exacerbated these feelings, and people have little time for each other in the family.

Muslim families have been fortresses of Muslim civilisation and in them women play their creative and decisive roles in a way which is complementary to men. When the Mongol onslaught overpowered Muslim lands in the 13th century CE, many Muslim women were forcibly married to the conquering soldiers. Within a generation the victors became captives of Islam, due mainly to the exemplary qualities of Muslim women.

Babies are born in a family fully dependent on the mercy of Allah whose most immediate agents are sometimes the parents. Their survival, and physical and personal growth are linked to their family members. In all these, the mother's role is vital. Throughout the history of Islam Muslim mothers have pioneered in passing on the body and spirit of Islam to following generations. Their self-esteem, confidence and pro-active and positive mothering produced generations of creative and dynamic Muslims.

If a Muslim woman is in worship and remembrance of her Lord, she is a solace to her husband and a refuge for her children. If she is fulfilled in her worship of Allah, she is a source of happiness in the family, and the sweetness, joy, peace and tranquillity in the house depend largely on her. She is a reservoir of strength and confidence for her husband and children. Islamic history is full of stories of valiant mothers who guided and encouraged their sons in their struggle for justice. The Arabic saying, 'the mother is a school' places women in their proper perspective. In the same way if a man is a slave and worshipper of Allah and is engaged in establishing the deen of Islam in the world, he is a source of strength to the woman and the children.

During the decadent period, some of the ummah lost the vitality of Islam and degenerated becoming sterile with women experiencing some of the worst of it. As their situation worsened, the fortress of the Muslim family started cracking. As a result, Muslims everywhere are now struggling to recover from their internal social haemorrhage. Unless Muslim family units, with women at the helm, are rejuvenated, the war to overcome Muslim impotence will be lost.

Historically, while women were denied their rights elsewhere, it was Islam that gave them dignity. Islam has confirmed man and woman in complementary, not competitive, roles in the family and in the society. Women are waived certain tasks, such as, the burden of earning for the family so they can devote their time, energies and intellects to the sound raising of healthy, intelligent, committed Muslim children. That does not preclude them from engaging in business or in any other suitable profession. In fact, Muslim communities everywhere desperately need educated and professional women. Umm al-Mu'minin Khadijah, the noble wife of the Prophet ﷺ, was a renowned businesswoman in her own right who before Islam appointed Muhammad ﷺ as her agent in trips to Syria.

The modern trend of 'the empowerment of women', invented to bring women into the labour market, as well as the tremendous economic pressures arising from the usurious economy, are putting physical and psychological pressure on women, including Muslim mothers, to go out and earn and build 'careers' at the expense of their commitment to the family. Of course, women may need engagement with work and economic matters in their lives. The issue here needs to be properly understood. What sort of engagement and what is the priority in life? Considering the physical pressure and psychological stress in maintaining balance between the family and professional life many 'career women' in the developed countries are now reducing their external commitments and returning to spend time with their children. After all, maintaining a house and rearing children are complete occupations in their own right. No one should be overburdened in life. Allah looks after the interests of both men and women. It is of course unfortunate that homemakers are still unrecognised and unremunerated in the developed societies, in spite of the language of equality and rights.

Allah does not impose on any self any more than it can stand. (Qur'an 2:286)

No burden bearer can bear another's burden. (Qur'an 35:18)

8. MUSLIM FAMILIES: FEATURES AND PURPOSES

Muslim families have some unique features. They guard against the wanderings of the sexual appetites and channel them within the wholesome and meaningful pursuit of life. They help with the increase of human virtues, such as, love, mercy, self-sacrifice and justice. They also provide a refuge from emotional and psychological disturbances of their members.[1] When families are centred on the worship and remembrance of Allah, they can be anchors of security and stability for human beings.

Muslim families have always been a source of inspiration for their members. In the earliest days of Islam, during the time of the Prophet ﷺ and in the following two generations, Muslim families played their most creative roles in the history of humankind.

The admirable military generals, political strategists, intellectual leaders, scholars, traders – all sincere teachers of Islam – were the products of blessed Muslim families. In that, Muslim women played an outstanding role.

The family is the microcosm of a society and, as such, there are distinct roles for its members, as mentioned in the following hadith:

> Each one of you is a trustee (shepherd) and is accountable for that which is entrusted to him. A ruler is trustee and is accountable for his trust, a man is a trustee in respect of his family, a woman is a trustee in respect of her husband's house and children. (*Sahih al-Bukhari* and *Muslim*).

As the elementary unit of an organised group life, a family has a leader, just as the society must have a leader. The Creator of human beings has placed man in that leadership role within the family context and prescribed that women remain loyal to men, just as Allah prescribes that Muslim men are obedient and loyal to Muslim leaders. In the first two-member family Adam was designated as the leader.

> Men are in charge of women, because Allah has made the one of them to excel the other, and because they spend of their property (for the support of women). So good are the obedient, guarding in secret that which Allah has guarded. (Qur'an 4:34).

> ... And they (women) have rights similar to those (of men) over them in kindness, and men are a degree above them. Allah is Mighty, Wise. (Qur'an 2:228)

These *ayat* of the Qur'an on the issue of leadership in the family have been misunderstood by many. Proponents of the radical feminist movement have attacked the 'inequality' of man and woman in Islam with a view to undermining Muslim family structure.

Divine wisdom guides every Islamic ruling. A common-sense understanding based on human physiology and emotion will justify the fairness of the man-woman relationship in Islam. Over 1400 years ago Allah, exalted is He, eliminated the status of women as 'chattels', prohibited the pre-Islamic practice of female infanticide and gave women full control over their own earnings and wealth. Allah has granted other rights to women, such as, the right of inheritance, the right to initiate divorce and the right to earn or own a business. The wife of the Prophet Muhammad ﷺ, Umm al-Mu'minin Khadijah, was one of the first to accept Islam. The first shaheed in Islamic history was also a woman. The Qur'an has clarified that men and women are indispensable partners in human civilisation.

"The believers, men and women, are protectors, one of another..." (Qur'an 9:71).

The distribution of responsibility in a family setting is to make sure that human society is saved from chaos and disorder. In any human organisation individuals know their duties and their boundaries. To Allah, no human being is superior to other, except in *taqwa*.

Men and women who are Muslims, men and women who are muminun, men and women who are obedient, men and women who are truthful, men and women who are steadfast, men and women who are humble, men and women who give sadaqa, men and women who fast , men and women who guard their private parts, men and women who remember Allah much: Allah has prepared forgiveness for them and an immense reward. (Qur'an 33:35)

The noblest among you in Allah's sight is the one with the most taqwa. Allah is All-Knowing, All-Aware. (Qur'an 49:13)

Leadership in the family context means that a husband has the responsibility for making the major decisions concerning the family's deen and well-being, after consultation with his wife or wives. That includes decisions on all aspects of the implementation of the *deen*, responsibility for his family' upbringing and education in the *deen*, as well as the worldly decisions on earning a halal income and maintaining the family. This latter is not only a moral but also a legal obligation. But he has no legal right over his wife's earnings, which are her own, unless she decides to spend for the family. Her priority is to look after her husband's property, their home and children, particularly with respect to a proper upbringing for the children in the *deen*. Conscientious husbands and wives work in consultation with each other in family affairs, but a wife is obliged to recognise her husband's right to lead the family, just as the husband may be consulted by his amir but must recognise and abide by the amir's decisions. Right-acting husbands and wives fear Allah and do not transgress the boundaries set by Him.[2]

> The Prophet ﷺ said: The best woman is she who, when you see her you feel pleased, and when you direct her she obeys. She protects your rights and keeps her chastity when you are absent. (*Ibn Majah*)

9. Rights and Responsibilities in the Family

Rights and responsibilities are intertwined. One's responsibility is the other's right. The rights and responsibilities of husbands, wives, parents and children are inscribed in the Shari'ah. When they are fully complied with, families secure heavenly peace and make a positive impact on societies.

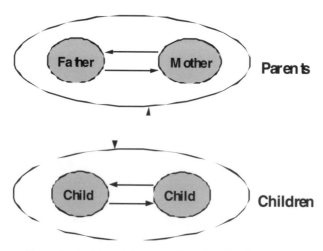

Figure 9.1 Rights and Responsibilities in a family unit

In extended families, these rights and responsibilities stretch over generations of people connected together by blood or marriage. A general principle is that older people deserve respect, but have more responsibility.

Among parents

As husband and wife, parents in the family have rights over each other. Islam has asked a Muslim wife to observe the following:

- she should be thankful to Allah, a part of which is being grateful to her husband, as it is mentioned in a hadith that most of the women in the Fire are those who are ungrateful.
- she should preserve her chastity.
- when her husband wants her physical company she should not refuse.
- she should look after the house and children effectively.

And also without her husband's permission she should not:
- give charity from his property.
- fast an optional fast.
- leave the house.
- invite into the house individuals, especially males, of whom he disapproves.

On the other hand, from her husband a wife has the right to:
- love
- respect
- fair treatment and
- dignified maintenance

In a Muslim family, husbands should be considerate and far from haughty. As husbands, the Prophet Muhammad ﷺ should be their role model.

Between Parents and Children

It is incumbent on parents to provide their children with basic human necessities – such as food, clothing, shelter, love, affection, upbringing and to take care of their health. This is treated as an *'ibadah* for the parents. It is also important for parents to teach their children courtesy, and to treat them with respect, and give them security, warmth and compassion. Above all, as human beings comprised of body and spirit, parents must provide their children with important life skills and spiritual nourishment. All these are rights of children in Shari'ah. Qur'an refers to a wise sage, Luqman, who exhorted his son on this (Qur'an 31:13-19).

The following hadith also speak of parental responsibility to the children:

> A father can give his child nothing better than good manners. (*At-Tirmidhi*)

> Be careful to your duty to Allah and be fair and just to your children. (*Sahih al-Bukhari*)

> Whoever properly brings up two daughters until they reach maturity, that man and myself (the Prophet ﷺ) will be as close in Paradise as two adjacent fingers. (*Sahih Muslim*)

On the other hand, children have their share of responsibilities to their parents. They can never repay their debts to their parents. However, they should try to reciprocate by helping them out in times of necessity, especially in their frailty. They should help parents in household chores and in any other work asked by them. They must not use such language or show attitudes towards parents that hurt them. Their gratitude to their parents, especially to their mothers who bore so much burden for them, is a divine requirement (Qur'an 2:83, 4:36, 17:23-24, 29:8, 31:14, 46:15).

There are many hadith regarding children's responsibilities toward their parents. The following are some of them:

> Allah's Messenger ﷺ said thrice, "Shall I not inform you of the biggest of the great wrong actions?" We said, "Yes, Messenger of Allah." He said, "To join partners in worship of Allah, to be ungrateful to one's parents. ..." (*Sahih al-Bukhari*)

> A man came to the Messenger of Allah ﷺ and asked permission to go on jihad. The Prophet ﷺ asked him, "are your parents alive?" The man said, "yes". The Prophet ﷺ responded, "then strive to

serve them." (*Sahih al-Bukhari* and *Muslim*)

A man came to the Prophet ﷺ and asked, "Who among people is most entitled to kind treatment from me?" He answered, "Your mother." The man asked, "Then who"? He said, "Your mother." "Then who"?, the man asked. The Prophet ﷺ said, "Your mother." The man asked, "Then who." The Prophet ﷺ said, "Then your father." (*Sahih al-Bukhari* and *Muslim*)

Paradise lies at the feet of your mother. (*An-Nasa'i*)

A father's pleasure is Allah's pleasure, a father's displeasure is Allah's displeasure. (*At-Tirmidhi*)

Among Children

Children are the flowers in a family garden. Although they carry the same parental 'blood' in them and carry many similar characteristics, all of them are different and unique. As flowers in a garden with varieties of colour and smell increase its beauty, children with varieties of physical and mental characteristics make the family elegant. Some children in the family become vocal, loud, vibrant and impulsive and the others become reflective, mature and quiet. These unique features of individuals make families with children blessed. Of course, many of the personality traits grow and take shape due to situational influence.

Whatever the differences within individuals in a family, parents and all the children enjoy and learn from one another. Children have their mutual rights and responsibilities. Obviously, from an Islamic point of view, elders have more responsibilities than the youngsters in a family. The elder brothers or sisters have a special place of respect in relation to the younger ones as well. In terms of respect they are next to parents. They often help the younger brothers and sisters grow through their experiences of life and the younger ones generally look to them as role models. They help the younger ones in education and transmitting life skills to them. They sometimes take them to school, parks and other places of interest. They play with them and give them invaluable joy in life. In any case, they become the effective educators or mentors of their brothers and sisters. When parents find things difficult to communicate with the younger ones they come forward and bridge the gap.

The younger ones are asked to listen to their elders and respect them. This love and respect come out naturally, and cannot be forcibly demanded. Sibling arguments, complaints or even fights are the signs of liveliness in the family, unless they create nuisance or danger. In most cases, the elders should be able to handle them with maturity and authority. Together they have a collective role, i.e., grow up as Muslims and maintain the dignity of the family.

10. IMPORTANT ISSUES ON FAMILY

The Spirit of Extended Family

Families, clans and tribes have been the sources of prestige and sociopolitical and economic status in the past and in many societies even today. Extended families, in which three or more generations live under the same family-umbrella, help Muslims to acquire many social qualities, such as self-sacrifice, compromise for the sake of the common good, mutual respect, affection and mutual consultation. Human beings are always inter-dependent. The nature of their dependence on others as babies or as frail elders may be different, but is in principle the same.

> When We grant long life to people, We return them to their primal state (back to weakness after strength). So will you not use your intellect? (Qur'an 36:67)

Old age is a feared reality of life. Imam Abu Hanifa, an intellectual giant in early Islam, was once heard to make a thoughtful remark on this that meant (sic) – 'when you first see grey hairs in your head welcome the new phase of your life'. It can be a painful stage of life where human beings, after passing through an era of physical strength and mental agility, may lose their grip on themselves and their surroundings. The supplication of Caliph Umar ؊ for the death of a martyr for himself before the frailty of old age reflected his wisdom. After a life of strength it is painful to be dependent on others even if it is on the children who were once reared with immense love and pain.

But, old age is by no means meaningless. It is the phase of wisdom in one's life and as such can be of enormous help in the extended family. It is common humanity that old people are looked after by the younger generation. It is a primary responsibility of a family. If, for some reasons, families fail, the society should become the safety net. It is cruel and inhuman that young and capable children would enjoy their life, while their parents carry the burden of 'old age' on their own or live in old people's home under social care. Children, who would definitely have perished without the support and love from their parents in their own childhood, have the responsibility to do the same for their parents when they need it most.

The virtue in the extended family arises from this humane attitude towards life. An extended family is like a miniature society where the wisdom of the elders, vitality of the youth and liveliness of the children keep buzzing and create a sense of togetherness among the members. There may be some natural difficulties and hardship in this arrangement, such as lack of privacy and individual space, but with good planning and considerate leadership they can be minimised. Moreover, experiencing some hardship is important for success in life.

In an extended family it is not necessary that all should live under the same roof. It depends on the economic ability of the family. The whole philosophy is to share with, care for and support each other. If properly managed, children from extended families learn better and are better equipped with vital social skills than others. The grandparents are also excellent educators and 'child-minders' in times of necessity. Extended families in Muslim societies have produced superior results compared to the 'nuclear family' structure of modern industrialised societies.

Goodness in the extended family – The experience of a family close to me has given me insight into the blessing of an extended family. They are a huge family, consisting of grandparents, married sons and daughters with their own children (grandchildren) and some yet unmarried children living as extended family members. They cannot live under one roof, because of the scarcity of large affordable housing in the metropolitan cities of Britain. But all the sons and daughters live close by and under one leadership, the grandfather. In his late sixties he still has a full grip on family affairs. Every adult is busy with job, study or business. He guides them, helps them when needed and decides, with consultation, on important aspects of the family. The sons and daughters listen to him, respect him and give him full support. The most prominent feature in the family is everybody's healthy interaction, not only among themselves, but with anyone who mixes with them. If people visit any of them, they immediately realise that they are the guests of everyone in the family. Even the young children, who are normally busy in their own world of play, come, greet them and talk to them with warmth. "This is amazing", said one of his friends who has been struggling to imbue some social qualities in his own children.

He is getting older and weaker. So, on one occasion I asked him, "What do you think is going to happen when you cannot lead any more"?

He was not so sure. "There will be natural separation, but I believe they will cling together, insha'Allah. The necessity of staying together is far more important in the permissive societies than in the Muslim lands", he commented.

I was amazed at his insight. If Muslims in the West could follow elders like him in this regard, a lot of our fears would have gone.

Domestic Violence

With sexual mayhem leading to increasing teenage pregnancy in many Western countries, boys and girls are becoming parents without acquiring the necessary sense of responsibility and accountability in life. In most cases their relationship is only skin deep. There is little plan for a long-term family bond. It is in the nature of materialism that it gives rise to a pseudo-individualism and superficial desire to enjoy, which is making it hard for people to live under the same roof for a length of time. As such, marriage is losing its importance as a permanent relationship between man and woman, divorce is increasing at an alarming rate and simply living together as 'partners' is becoming a norm. While ostentatious love-making in public places is ample, husbands and wives or unmarried partners argue, fight and abuse each other at home. This 'public lovey-dovey and private squabble' is on the increase. Once again, women suffer the worst. It has been reported that, in Britain, more and more men are beating women at home. The result is distressing to children who are caught in the crossfire of this family squabble, and who become pawns in the family disintegration and thus create problems in schools and on the streets. The rising juvenile delinquency and youth criminality in the developed countries do have strong links with family difficulties – mistrust between fathers and mothers, their feuds, domestic violence and abuse at home.

From a report by 'Family Policy Studies Centre' in Britain a frightful picture was published in the *Guardian* of London (27 March 2000) with the title, 'Are we turning into a nation of loners?' about family issues in Britain. It is disturbing that 38% of babies are born outside marriage (compared to only 7.2% in 1964), the number of lone parents has trebled from 7% in 1972 to 21% and more British people are getting used to living 'solo'. The percentages of all these are increasing every year.

Unfortunately, Muslims are also being gradually sucked into this social black hole. Family help-lines run by Muslims in recent years have recorded that verbal and physical abuse within Muslim families is on the rise. The causes of the abuse are linked to drug and substance abuse, extra-marital affairs, unemployment-related frustration, media influence, free-mixing of the sexes outside the home, interference of the in-laws, etc. Moreover, some cultural Muslims treat their wives strictly in the name of Islam. Their understanding of women's right is very shallow and they only adopt rigidity in dealing with their womenfolk, as if women are only meant to serve them at home and cook food for everyone. Although the true message of Islam is gaining momentum, ignorance still costs a great deal in terms of Muslim family life.

Fostering and Adoption

'Fostering' means taking care of someone else's children when their own parents have died or are unable to look after them for various reasons. The Prophet Muhammad ﷺ himself was fostered in his childhood according to the Makkan custom, although his mother was still alive. At a later period, he treated his foster-mother, Halima, with the highest esteem. The world is such a place that few things in life are certain. Allah, the Lord of the universe, has kept destiny in His own Hands. Accidents, sudden death, poverty, war – can make children orphans or throw them into appalling and tragic conditions. According to UNHCR, Muslims now constitute most of the refugee population in the world.

Nowadays, governments or social care agencies arrange families that can look after orphans and give them good homes. 'Adoption' is a step ahead of fostering and has legal implications as well. Fostering and adoption require parental roles to be undertaken by persons who are not the children's biological parents. Adopted children are supposed to enjoy similar privileges to natural children. Through adoption, a couple who are not blessed with children of their own have the chance to raise children. This helps them emotionally.

Whatever the reason, Islam has strongly advised Muslims to foster children in need and look after them properly. They should be treated with the best of kindness and love. Social and economic chaos in many Muslim countries is pushing huge number of Muslim children on the mercy of NGOs (Non-Governmental Organisation) run by non-Muslims. There is genuine concern that many of them will grow up without a basic Islamic background. Muslim communities in the West thus have a tremendous responsibility in sharing some of the burdens of the ummah in this regard.

In Islam, fostering or adoption does not make children sons or daughters. The law of inheritance does not apply to them. However, they are to be loved, cared and raised in the same way as one's biological children. The Qur'an has given the guidelines on this in the following way

> ... nor has He (Allah) made your adopted sons your actual sons. These are just words by your mouths. But Allah speaks the truth

and He guides to the Way. Call them after their fathers. That is closer to justice in Allah's sight. But if you do not know their fathers' name, then they are your brothers in faith and people under your patronage. (Qur'an 33:4-5)

11. MODERN THREATS TO THE FAMILY

Families in the West are now facing challenges from many quarters. With increased pressure to survive and succeed, human beings are unfortunately compromising with their inner selves and with the higher values of life. Since the industrial revolution women have been required to take part in economic activities. As the balance in the gender role tilted, it became the turning point in the family and social dynamics. During the Second World War, as millions of young men fought and died, more women were thrown into the world of work. The proponents of materialistic ideas took this further and started defining women's role as 'competitive' rather than 'complementary' and in terms of 'equality' rather than 'equity'. The imbalance in gender roles thus has a negative influence on the attitude toward marriage, family, conception and often now results in abortion of the foetus. The liberalisation of attitude toward sex is now expanding its frontier, opening the floodgates to many aberrant sexual practices, and the modern West is moving further away form its Judaeo-Christian roots.

The marriage-based family has been threatened with a number of alternatives in the western societies, e.g., cohabitation, single-parenthood and homosexuality.

a) Cohabitation

As marriage is becoming less popular, it is gradually being replaced by cohabitation which means couples live with each other without being legally married. Cohabitation, even in the recent past, was a temporary phenomenon. But, it has been observed that couples are now spending more time in cohabitation. They may or may not marry in the end. Why many people are leaving aside marriage as a social norm and adopting cohabitation is a complex question. Obviously, there are historical, moral, social and economic factors. The weakening of religious or spiritual values in people, fear of the burden of a long-term commitment to marriage, unwillingness to compromise and sacrifice for another person, the growing opportunities for women to develop lives for themselves outside marriage, the removal of the stigma on 'unmarried mothers' and 'illegitimate children' with the social acceptance of cohabitation and the recognition of children born out of wedlock are some of the main factors for this increase.

b) Single-parenthood

The reason for single-parenthood could be the death of one spouse, divorce, separation, desertion by one partner or result from a deliberate choice. There could be economic and other factors in people choosing to remain single-parents. The vast majority of single-parents are women. The rise in single-parenthood is linked with the increase in the divorce rate and also to an increase in births outside marriage. As society is adjusting to this 'emerging form' of the family, it is gradually being treated as a norm.

The issue of single-parent families is of major concern in the West because of its social and economic cost. With only one parent around, children grow under the care of half parenting. The vital component of the other half is missing. This has an emotional effect as well. In most cases, one parent cannot cope with earning a livelihood and looking after the whole child at the same time. This puts single parents at a perpetual disadvantage in society. In general, single-parenthood is associated with low living standards.

Most researches have shown that there are social and psychological effects on children raised in single-parent families. They are more likely to grow emotionally disturbed and become delinquent and engage in crime and drug abuse. Single-parenthood seems to have an effect on the rising number of children with

Emotional and Behavioural Difficulties (EBD) in schools and on juvenile criminality in many inner city deprived areas.

c) Homosexuality

The family is now being redefined in many countries in the West. On 28th October 1999, the British House of Lords ruled that "a homosexual couple in a stable relationship can be defined as a family". As a result, a former Royal Navy serviceman was entitled to inherit the tenancy of his late male partner's flat. In recent decades gay rights' lobbies have been wielding much influence in the political arena of many Western countries. They are gradually making inroads by pushing homosexuality as being a normal lifestyle, at par with normal marriage and family life. Are the children of Adam going to accept such a practice that invited Allah's displeasure in the past?

12. THE PROSELYTISATION AND THE CHALLENGE

Being in the driving seat of world affairs, Western countries wield tremendous influence in the rest of the world, not only in politics and economics, but in moral and cultural values as well. The UN, effectively run by Western powers, has also become the instrument of the post-modern secular worldview. The unbalanced concept of man-woman relationship, marriage, family and women's rights promoted by proselytising secularists is now being pushed forward for acceptance by the rest of the world through the UN-sponsored programme of 'women empowerment'. It is no surprise that this programme is resented by the rest of humanity because of its inherent flaws. There is a passionate defiance to this proselytising tendency. Humankind cannot afford to give in to this extreme liberal view which paves the way to disastrous consequences for human beings.

Surely, women suffered in history, as have men. Deviation from divine truth, using religion as a cover to oppress women and women's lack of confidence in standing up to injustice in the past all played their part. However, over the millennia many champions of human rights, prophets and other sages, fought for gender equity within the institution of the family. The advent of Islam ushered in a new era with a dignified position for women in the world. Families, on the basis of justice and respect for both men and women, proved to be the sources of Muslim glory. Muslim families became the centres of the mundane and spiritual meaning of life, and a life-long school. Muslim children were moulded by the universal nature of Islam, as they grew with confidence in the value-rich family environment. But, unfortunately, due to the political and intellectual sterility of parts of the Muslim world in the last few centuries, human beings have virtually lost a balanced view of life in all these matters. In the post-modern moral maze, all values related to human life, e.g., marriage, family, sex, etc., are now losing their ethical and spiritual dimensions. It is a nightmare scenario for this planet Earth and it looks as if the future of the human species is on test.

It is encouraging that in recent times there has been a growing sense of urgency in bringing back the moral and ethical dimensions in the debate on marriage and family. Many high-flying career men and women are now realising that family is more than career and prosperity, and that life on earth is too precious to be measured in terms of fame and wealth. Children and family are now once again coming into the social debate. This realisation is bringing people from various communities and faith groups together. This needs to be given further momentum. Muslim communities in the West should come forward pro-actively to forge alliances with pro-family people in order to save this institution from further erosion. Family building should now be the battleground in the long drawn fight against the brutal oppression of materialism.

NOTES

[1] *Women in Islam* by Aisha Lemu & Fatima Heeren, p38, The Islamic Foundation, UK, 1978

[2] *Women in Islam* by Aisha Lemu & Fatima Heeren, p18, The Islamic Foundation, UK, 1978

3. Blessed Family and Nation Building

Executive Summary – Part Three

- HAPPY AND SPIRITUALLY SUCCESSFUL FAMILIES with solid human values can produce good human beings. However, the ultimate destiny belongs to Allah Who can bring good human beings out of the worst situations and produce disbelievers out of the best situations. A good family can bring a sense of belonging, anchor and roots and build balanced beings in children, who can then contribute to society. Children growing up in these families can be equipped with the necessary tools to create blessed societies.

- Happy and blessed families have essential ingredients, e.g., love, mercy, respect, loyalty, forgiveness, sacrifice, fairness, honesty and openness, etc. Their absence from any family or society is disastrous. In the midst of injustice, oppression and vengeance, the world cannot afford the weakening of the institution of the family.

- In addition, Muslim families should be reservoirs of knowledge and learning. Islamic principles and the acts of worship should be openly practised so that children can simply make them their life habits. The family environment should carry a positive message and leave an imprint of the Islamic ethos.

- The family environment should be free of dry and lifeless

practices. A lively and open environment with freedom of thought produces confidence in children who do not feel any inhibition in expressing themselves and acting pro-actively.

- Muslims have to watch out for pitfalls, so that no one in the family falls through the net. Supplication for children by parents and vice-versa is pleasing to Allah and is psychologically rewarding. It blends the relationship between them and creates love for each other.

13. INGREDIENTS OF A BLESSED FAMILY

Our Lord, give us joy in our spouses and children and make us a good example for those who have taqwa. (Qur'an 25:74)

The family, being the bedrock of human society, is a noble institution and as such it universally needs to be preserved. It should not only be defended robustly, but should be promoted with passion and conviction. In the midst of the 'anti-family' movement by a small, but powerful, section of die-hard secularists in the developed world the challenge has become all the more important. The promotion or rejection of family values is linked to the perception of life on earth and the role of man and woman in human history. Those who have a firm belief in divine revelation cannot conceive of weakening the family structure.

If the relationship between a man and a woman is built on transitory infatuation and romance or the attitude of 'having a nice time', it cannot form families because they need long-term commitment, responsibility and mature decisions about life. Such people could not even 'plan' to marry, let alone have children within wedlock. Marriage and families connect people to each other and anchor them in a life-long commitment. It is hard for short-sighted and selfish people to look beyond immediate pleasure, and thus they degrade themselves with the passion for mere physical satisfaction. Even if they form families they end up in recrimination and tears within a short period. An unhappy family creates disaffection, pain and frustration that give rise to crushed personalities full of confusion. Distortion in family leads toward 'distorted personality'. Young people raised in unhappy families can turn out to be dangers to society and even to humanity. Dysfunctional families rob children of their happiness.

On the contrary, a happy family is the reservoir of positive parenting. It brings a sense of belonging, anchor and roots that build balanced personalities within children, who then contribute positively to the society. Children growing up in blessed families are equipped with the tools to create blessed societies. The following are the major ingredients of blessed families. The list is not exhaustive.

THE INGREDIENTS

Love

Love is at the core of family life. It can achieve things that cannot be achieved by force. Love captivates, influences, and moves things to happen. It penetrates deep into the self. It is the gel that produces a rock-solid relationship among people. Love is imbedded in human nature and a gift from Allah. Human history has exceptional stories on love. Love is power and as such has the capacity to build or burn human societies. Love emanates from the core of the heart. Hearts join and create fountains of love between two people, the father and mother. The arrival of a child in the family makes this love intense. As such, 'Father And Mother, I Love You' is an excellent acronym of FAMILY.

Love for one's own children is obvious, as they are a blessed product of physical love between a man and a woman. Obviously, love between a husband and wife, two grown up people with two distinct personalities, needs careful nurturing from both. Pure physical attraction cannot create love or maintain it for long, although in a marriage this is important. Attraction before marriage that gives rise to romance and an 'unacceptable' relationship often fails in the test and ends up in marital breakdown. People looking for family life have the rewards of permanent

53

love on their side. They have the best chance of success. An Islamic vision of life in the family makes love exceptionally rewarding. In any situation, the 'joining' of hearts is due to Allah's special blessing. Wealth and beauty are not to be despised, but they cannot buy love.

> And (as for the believers) Allah has unified their hearts. If you had spent everything on the earth you could not have unified their hearts, but Allah has unified them. He is Almighty, All Wise. (Qur'an 8:63).

> Some people set up equals to Allah, loving them as they should love Allah. But those who have iman have greater love for Allah. (Qur'an 2:165).

> Say: 'If your fathers or your sons or your brothers or your wives or your tribe, or any wealth you have acquired, or any business you fear may slump, or any house which pleases you, are dearer to you than Allah and His Messenger and doing jihad in His Way, then wait until Allah brings about His command. Allah does not guide people who are deviators.' (Qur'an 9:24)

Love between parents is a reservoir where children find their sanctuary, if that love results from a higher love of Allah and His Messenger ﷺ. Parental love transmits naturally to children. Lack of even the minimum of love between parents may be the cause of emotional disturbance in the children. 'Child abuse' in many families has something to do with mechanical or loveless parenting and children growing in that family environment lack the necessary emotional skills to cope with the emptiness in their lives. Many may succumb to juvenile delinquency and anti-social behaviour.

Love has external manifestations and that is natural. But, love between two adult people should not be so ostentatious that it becomes indecent and provocative in the public eye.

Mercy

Mercy is at the heart of family and social life. Allah, "Most Gracious, Most Merciful" (Qur'an 1:2), has created man out of His mercy and demands from us the same. The Qur'an has also used the word rahmah (mercy) to describe the relationship among Muslims.

> Muhammad is the Messenger of Allah; and those who are with him are strong against unbelievers, (but) full of mercy among themselves. (Qur'an 48:29)

In a Muslim family, because of the actual relationship and the presence of Islam, the manifestation of mercy among its members is more pronounced. The Prophet Muhammad ﷺ was the symbol of mercy to his family, his companions, the ummah of Muslims, mankind at large and the universe, for as Allah says:

> We have only sent you as a mercy to all the worlds. (Qur'an 21:107)

> Have mercy on those in the land, so that the One in Heaven will have mercy on you. (*Sunan al-Tirmidhi*)

> Allah is kind and He loves kindness in all affairs. (*Sahih al-Bukhari* and Muslim).

> He who is deprived of leniency is deprived of goodness (*Sahih Muslim*)

> When Allah, the Exalted, wills some good towards the people of a household, He introduces kindness among them. (*Musnad, Sahih al-Ja'mi*).

> Allah loves kindness and rewards it in such away that He does not reward for harshness or anything else. (*Sahih Muslim*)

Children deprived of mercy in their childhoods are being punished for no fault of their own. Parental indifferences and ill temper destroy their childhood and may rob them of future happiness.

Respect and Honour

> He is not of us who has no compassion for our little ones and does not honour our old ones. (*At-Tirmidhi*)

Human beings are the manifestation of the divine will, and Allah has breathed spirit into each of them. Each one of us ought to show due respect to the other. Every human being has the potential of doing something, although some are obviously more capable than others. The test in this world is to see who can maximise their efforts to the best of their ability and for the pleasure of Allah. The act of respect is the recognition of that worth. Respect is reciprocal – if someone is given respect, there is every likelihood that the other will reciprocate that. Allah expects Muslims to show respect to each other.

Each child grows with certain personality traits. Even twin brothers or sisters each have unique characteristics. Respect for an individual is thus natural and brings happiness. We all learn from each other, even from tiny babies. Everyone has views on different aspects of life. Respect for each other's knowledge and freedom of expression give rise to fellow feeling, motivation and creativity. The formulation and expression of knowledge depend on family and social environment.

Even though family members may live under the same roof, each person has a world of their own that needs to be respected. As children grow older, they need to learn the etiquette of a Muslim house. As an example, Islam teaches decency, and family is the first institution where they should learn it. Islam requires members of the household to seek permission when entering each other's rooms. Parents, of course, need to know what is happening in their children's worlds and should endeavour to implement a positive ethos with full honesty and without being intrusive and insensitive. Like everyone else, children need their own space and time. Conscientious parents leave a lot of space for them so that they grow with self-respect and respect for others, especially for older people including elder brothers and sisters.

Members of a family are expected to maintain the honour of the family by their positive behaviour and defending it from external threat. Islam considers it a disgrace if people undermine their own family. However, that honour should be based on Islamic spirit, not any other thing, e.g. tribalism.

Loyalty

Loyalty has a relational aspect and a wider meaning. The minimum requirement in a family is that husband and wife must be loyal to each other in their marital relationship. Infidelity in marriage is a grave wrong action, punishable in the harshest manner. While fidelity is rewarding in both worlds, infidelity brings suspicion, mental torture, frustration and a 'hellish' atmosphere in this world and a real Hell in the Hereafter unless Allah turns to one in forgiveness. Loyalty to each other in the family is enhanced by love and respect.

A family is bonded by marriage and blood relationship and is one of the keys to group life. Family loyalty thus gives a part of the identity of a member of the family.

However, without a proper understanding this can create narrow sense of pride and produce 'family feuds' as is often seen in many societies. A family blends together through loyalty and trust among its members to create a wider unit. In the history of humankind, family loyalty grew into tribal loyalty and created kingdoms and civilisations on the one hand and destroyed them on the other. *'Asabiya* (or familial and tribal loyalty) was at the heart of pre-Islamic Arab character. Islam refined its dynamic and powerful features with a view to creating a community, the ummah. Its potent force held sway and created an unparalleled dynamism in the history of mankind, as shown by Ibn Khaldun.

Patience and Forgiveness

People living close together, with shared space and other material resources, need understanding, compromise and sacrifice. Human beings have both 'evil and good' traits in their character (Qur'an 91:8) and as such have innate strengths and weaknesses. Close people, parents and children, living under the same roof definitely experience this in each other. Intelligent are those who acknowledge, understand and overlook the weaknesses and live with them, unless they are serious. Of course, we all need to improve ourselves and try sensitively to improve others. But negative features of family members and others should not occupy our minds. Those who can see things positively live in peace and harmony. Cynics often suffer and intolerant people lose out. They are the source of dissension in the society. The reasons for family breakdown in many cases are due to the lack of compromise on smaller issues. Insensitive and sometimes silly comments and counter comments raise tension between family members leading to arguments and shouting matches. A wonderful piece of advice from the Qur'an can put things into perspectives.

> Live together with them correctly and courteously. If you dislike them, it may well be that you dislike something in which Allah has placed a lot of good. (Qur'an 4:19)

A family or a society remains divided and can even break up in recrimination if patience and forgiveness get thinner among its members. These are the qualities of big hearts that bring immense reward from Allah (see Qur'an 3:159, 7:199, 42:43). Patience is a great quality that needs to be sought from Allah (see Qur'an 2:153).

Sacrifice

> But (they) give preference over themselves, even though they themselves are needy. And who so is saved from his own avarice – such are they who are successful. (Qur'an 59:9)

Sacrifice has many dimensions. Spending of time, energy and wealth in the Way of Allah is the highest mission in life for a Muslim. It emanates from a conscious understanding of what it means. Sacrifice is an inescapable ingredient in the world of creating a Islamic civilisation. It is linked to self-surrender to Allah and the fullest conviction in Islam. It is an essential building block that builds individuals' characters in order that they may play meaningful roles on earth. The sacrifice of the earlier generations of Islam, in the wake of apparently insurmountable barriers, was the stepping stone for the ascendancy of Islam. The history of humankind teaches one single message, e.g., sacrifice is at the core of victory.

The primary sacrifice starts in a family, where a mother sacrifices her comforts during pregnancy. Nine months of carrying a growing foetus in the womb, being ever watchful that it is properly nourished inside and saved from harm, prepares her for more sacrifice when the baby is born. Her eating habits, sleep, rest, work – are all programmed for the tiny creature. Throughout infancy, both father and mother willingly re-organise their lives, day after day, to adjust themselves to the needs of the little baby. As the child grows, the necessity for sacrifice takes different forms. Every time a new baby arrives in the house their sacrifices multiply. Unfortunately, the fear of this sacrifice has guided some people to avoid children altogether or limit their number for selfish reasons.

Earning for the family and spending on its members cannot happen without the spirit of sacrifice. Parents often sacrifice their careers, work harder and earn more money only to bring comfort to their children, pay for a good education and attempt to guarantee successful lives for them. But modern materialistic men and women are tempted to earn and spend for themselves alone, so that no one can demand a share of their 'good life'. The burden of family seems too much for them. This is why we sometimes see fathers running away from their responsibilities and mothers dropping their innocent babies on the doorsteps or even in dustbins, in spite of all the support from the state.

Sacrificing one's opinions and ego is important for the success of family life. It is essential to achieve greater harmony in the community. Many people fail in this area. Muslims, of course, have strong views on the basic tenets of Islam, where there is no room for compromise. But those basic issues are only a few. Islam demands sacrifice for the wider benefit of human beings, their family, society, the ummah and, in fact, the whole of humanity.

Justice and Fairness

O you who believe, be steadfast witnesses for Allah in equity and let not the hatred of any people incite you to depart from justice.

> Be just, that is closer to piety… (Qur'an 5:8)
>
> Allah commands justice and doing good and giving to relatives, … (Qur'an 16:90)

Justice is at the heart of Allah's creative design. The creation of the Garden and the Fire is to bring about final justice, as the earthly life is too short to establish justice. The Arabic words, Qist and 'Adl are very wide indeed. They are intertwined with the implementation of Truth. The manifest balance and proportion in the creation is the reflection of Allah's justice in the universe. Maintaining proper balance between rights and responsibilities is the essence of justice.

Justice in the family does not necessarily mean equal shares in everything for everyone. In the real world, justice means equitable and balanced dealings. Most importantly, dealing in the family should not be 'seen' as unjust and unfair, especially by the children. We may not be fully aware, but children are keen observers of what happens around them and what their parents say or do. It is important that parents attain an extra degree of consciousness in their behaviour and dealings. The family is a mini-community and justice established there has an impact on the wider society.

Tiny things, little words and small actions matter to children. It is difficult to believe that Muslim parents would be unfair or unjust to one or the other child. But every child is different. One child may be more intelligent, has good observance of the deen, is always willing to listen or has some other qualities over the others. Moreover, a parent may prefer a boy or a girl for some emotional reasons. All these can invite special attention of a parent towards a particular child. The prophet Ya'qub ﷺ had a special liking for his beloved son Yusuf ﷺ over others for genuine reasons. What it means is that, even if parents are emotionally warmer towards one child, they should not visibly discriminate against others.

Consultation

Allah has commanded believers to conduct their affairs and settle their differences in consultation.

... So pardon them, and ask forgiveness for them and consult with them upon the conduct of affairs. And when you have reached a firm decision, put your trust in Allah.. Allah loves those who put their trust in Him. (Qur'an 3:159)

... and those who manage their affairs by mutual consultation...(Qur'an 42:38).

Consultation is in the spirit of social life, and the Prophet Muhammad ﷺ practised it in his domestic and public life. In order to teach his ummah the importance of consultation he even decided to go against his own view in some cases, e.g., in the battle of Uhud. During the treaty of Hudaybiya when the Muslims failed to comprehend the impending victory and were showing reluctance to follow his verbal instruction regarding the 'Umra (lesser pilgrimage) he consulted Umm Salama, his wife who was accompanying him, as to what to do. Her unique suggestion came as a blessing from Allah and healed all.

Bearing in mind that in the end the decision must be made by the head of the family or the amir of the community, yet consultation produces confidence, trust, interest, mutual respect and team spirit in a family. It enhances creativity and produces a responsible outlook among the members. It creates a sense of ownership in everybody's mind, which is essential for any venture to succeed. However, consultation needs diligence and relevance and should not go around in a circle. Proper decision making is important. If misconstrued, it could lead to indecision or no decision. Spirited consultation helps cure the diseases of arrogance and egotism. It is the pillar of a successful social life. In Islam consultation is the life-blood of social health.

Consultation in a family is essential for creating a positive and lively environment. It builds a bond between husband and wife. It helps them plan for the family, household chores and effective parenting. As children grow they should be involved in the process of consultation, particularly in affairs that affect them. It helps the whole family to sail through difficulties in modern life, as 'two brains are always better than one'. There is immense blessing in consultation.

Honesty and Integrity

> Surely truth leads to virtue and virtue leads to the Garden. (*Sahih al-Bukhari*)

> Guarantee me six things and I shall assure you of the Garden – When you speak, speak the truth; keep your promise; discharge your trust; guard your chastity: lower your gaze; and withhold your hands from highhandedness. (*Al-Bayhaqi*)

Honesty, integrity and trustworthiness are the essence of a Muslim. These are also basic leadership qualities. In a family context the father is the leader. Sons and daughters emulate their fathers and mothers as role models in different ways. Muslim parents thus need to be honest, not only because it makes them better parents but because they are accountable to Allah for their actions.

Parents are like shepherds at home. Honest and truthful parents create exemplary qualities in their children through words and deeds. The following story tells us how Muslim mothers trained the teachers of humanity.

Honesty has its fruit – Abd al-Qadir al-Jaylani is known as a great saint and teacher of Islam. He is also noted for his knowledge and wisdom. His father died when he was very young, so his righteous mother brought him up. Through Allah's mercy and by her efforts he grew up with a thirst for knowledge. As he was finishing his education in a local school the young Abd al-Qadir learnt that Baghdad was famous for its scholars and people of knowledge. With his mother's permission he decided to go there. When the time came he prepared for the journey and joined a caravan that was going to Baghdad. His mother gave him forty gold Dinars so that he could live independently in Baghdad and concentrate fully on education. As a precaution she sewed them into the lining of his clothes so that no one could see them or hear their noise. She also told him that whatever might happen to him he should never tell a lie, even if telling the truth would cost him his life.

On the way bandits attacked the caravan and all the people were robbed of their possessions. One of the bandits asked young Abd al-Qadir whether he had anything valuable with him. Abd al-Qadir, without hesitation said, "Yes, I have forty gold Dinars". They would not believe him in the beginning, but the innocent face of the boy said he was not telling a lie. "Where are they", asked the leader. "They are sewn into my clothes", replied Abd al-Qadir. They tore the lining of the clothes open and could see the shining Dinars. The bandit leader was overwhelmed by the truthfulness of the boy and asked, "Why did you tell us about the money?" "My mother advised me never to tell a lie, even if speaking the truth would cost my life. How could I disregard her?", replied the boy without any fear or sense of loss.

The leader was taken aback, thought for a while and looked at his gang. Everybody was speechless. A feeling of remorse attacked him from inside. How could he rob people when he knew perfectly well that what he was doing was completely wrong? His instinct was telling him to repent, and he did so immediately asking his men to return everything they had stolen.[1]

Openness and Clarity

The implementation of Islam created societies where openness and transparency, on one hand, and accountability, on the other, worked hand in hand. Muslims abhor suspicion and spying on each other, in the family and in the society. They are not only unethical but criminal acts as well. They eat away the trust among people.

O you who believe, avoid most suspicion. Indeed some suspicion is a crime. And do not spy and do not backbite one another. (Qur'an 49:12)

When parents are open and forthright in their affairs and matters related with the family, it has a tremendous positive effect on the children. Children can easily relate to them, open their minds to them and discuss issues of importance. Openness may occasionally put parents on the spot, but this is how it should be. It gives more confidence to the children and in return makes the parents more self-aware. If parents happen to possess some undesired habits or are inclined to some wrong practices they must come up with a determined effort to stop them. Attempts to hide them may have serious negative consequences on the children's beings.

Openness and transparency generate virtue in the family. The personal and family life of the Prophet Muhammad ﷺ was in the full light of history, which, as a role model, illuminates Muslim life. Muslims hate double standard in personal and social life. A Muslim parent should never play 'Jekyll and Hyde' in his life, especially with his children.

> O you who believe, why do you say what you do not do? It is deeply abhorrent to Allah that you say what you do not do. (Qur'an 61:2-3)

14. A FAMILY ETHOS BASED ON VALUES

Establishment of an Islamic ethos in the house is the enviable asset of a Muslim family. It is a joint responsibility of both the father and the mother. Children growing up in a positive family and community environment have a strong anchor in life. They are generally positive contributors to society. Children, from their early years, need to be trained properly so that they become part of this learning process and can contribute to the family according to their age and maturity.

Islam has five unique pillars. The rites of prayer and fasting are open and done publicly and when parents practise them consistently children will inevitably follow them from their early childhood. Parents need to give extra effort to involving their young ones in social work, charity and other humanitarian works. Children should be taught about Eid festivals, Zakah, Hajj so that they are ingrained in their minds as they grow. As most in the West are eligible to pay Zakah and perform Hajj, they should be purposefully discharged in a way that children learn this from the points of view of the *deen* and society. The two Muslim celebrations give Muslim children invaluable opportunities to learn the essence of enjoyment in communal activities. They come to understand the bonding that Muslims wants to create among within the ummah. Children should be encouraged to take part in discussion on all these issues in a manner they understand. If the basic Islamic practices are carried out with real spirit at home they make a permanent impact on the children's personalities and future lives. They also create a dynamic and happy family environment.

Purification of the self and personal development are essential in a world where wrong action proliferates in society and stress tends to dominate our daily life. This needs continuous remembrance of Allah, steadfastness, perseverance and devoted prayer (Qur'an 7:205, 33:41-42). It also needs high spirit of mind, unrelenting Jihad (struggle) and selfless efforts to serve humanity for the sake of Allah. Our success on earth depends on purifying our selves (Qur'an 91:9).

A dynamic Muslim family continually strives to raise the spiritual elevation as well as the worldly success of its members. But human beings' success in the world and the Hereafter is fully dependent on Allah's blessing. No matter how professionally people plan and how hard they try, the result is with Allah. This is the spirit of Tawakkul (reliance on Allah) which protects human beings from the agony of uncertainty and fear of failure. "Allah loves those who put their trust (rely) on Him" (Qur'an 3:159).

Here comes the Islamic requirement of Du'a (supplication) to Allah, which, if properly done, fills the human heart with contentment, since Allah does answer the du'a in the time and the manner that are in accordance to His wisdom. The Messenger of Allah ﷺ has taught Muslims how to supplicate for good things at every moment and in hard times, such as after the painful events in Ta'if and during the heat of the battle of Badr. This he did even though he was a Prophet ﷺ and his past and future wrong act ions were forgiven.

Allah is angry with he who does not ask (anything) from Him. (*At-Tirmidhi*)

Supplication is the spirit of worship. (*At-Tirmidhi*)

Supplication for children by the parents and vice versa is pleasing to Allah and is rewarding psychologically. It produces joy in the mind and tranquillity in the heart. It creates love and respect for and loyalty to each other. In response to the special prayer of the prophet Ibrahim ﷺ (Qur'an 2:129), Allah promised the advent of Prophet Muhammad ﷺ. The Qur'an and the books of hadith contain supplications that should be practised by all in the family.

> Our Lord, give us joy in our spouses and children and make us a good example for those who have taqwa. (Qur'an 25:74)

> Lord, show mercy to them as they did in looking after me when I was little. (Qur'an 17:23-24)

In one hadith there are said to be three supplications that are answered – there being no doubt about it; the supplication of the oppressed, the supplication of the traveller and the supplication of the parent for the child. (*Ibn Majah*)

15. CHALLENGING THE IMPEDIMENTS!

A close-knit family with an Islamic ethos and a positive learning environment has the most likelihood of guarding everyone from evil – the evils of greed, selfishness, laxity and lust that thrive so rapidly, like viruses, in permissive societies. They are the impediments in human beings' journey towards Allah.

And then there are the threats that are haunting most parents today, Muslims and non-Muslim alike. The black hole of social diseases, negative peer pressure, etc, is causing mayhem in the society. Children are being 'lost' in the sea of whims and desires, sensuality and promiscuity, in a moral maze and a spiritual void. School phobia, truancy and disaffection are now becoming common, particularly with secondary-age children. This is giving rise to delinquency, gangsterism, drug and alcohol addiction, bullying and criminal activities in the inner cities in which most Muslims are concentrated. In the absence of role models, and with racial prejudice and religious discrimination, the lack of motivation and self-esteem are thwarting the potentials of many in the community. The sense of impotence in the midst of global injustice is making many fatalist.

The list of impediments is long. The challenge faced by parents in a family is enormous. Raising children in this social climate is becoming more demanding and parents need always to be on their guard. In spite of all their efforts in keeping everything in order, things can go wrong and tension and emotion can rise in the family. Human relationships are complex and often sensitive. Difficulties in a family most often start with small arguments, for whatever reasons, between husband and wife or between a child and parent. Petty arguments can create tension leading to conflict and anger. If not contained in time, anger may pile up and, like fire, it can burn the fabric of relationships in the family. Fortunately, most people are resilient in coping with their emotions.

As children grow, parental expectations of them rise. Parents look for obedience, discipline and a good output from their sons and daughters in almost everything. When this is not delivered or not seen to be delivered by the children, parents become disappointed and upset. Some parents become paranoid in the very first instance. Strong words are expressed, perhaps loudly, and things go wrong. Strong emotions are part of human nature and some are not that good in their expression. Many forget that while emotions in the right place and in the right manner are essential, they can be dangerous in the wrong place and wrong manner. Uncontrolled anger in the family is the recipe for disaster.

Muslim parents who want to create a new generation of capable Muslims for civilisational change themselves need a high level of behavioural management before they can train their younger ones. Conflicts do occur among human beings, but they must know how to resolve them. They are essential ingredients of parenting skills.

Those who spend in ease and adversity, those who control their rage and pardon other people – Allah loves the good-doers. (Qur'an 3:134)

Allah's Messenger ﷺ mentioned, "Some are swift to anger and swift to cool down, the one characteristic making up for the other; some are slow to anger and slow to cool down, the one characteristic making up for the other; but the best of you are those who are slow to anger and swift to cool down; and the worst of you are those who are swift to anger and slow to cool down". He continued, "Beware of anger, for it is a live coal in the heart of the descendants of Adam. Do you not notice the swelling of the vein of his neck and the redness of his eyes? So, when anyone experiences anything of that nature he should lie down and cleave to the earth." (*At-Tirmidhi*)

He is not strong who throws down another, but he [strong] is who control his anger. (*Sahih al-Bukhari* and Muslim)

NOTES

[1] from *Stories: Good and True for Children*, Translated by Matina Wali Muhammad, Ta-ha Publishers, London 1994.

Conclusion

Human beings crave hope and success. They need them in their personal lives, in their families and in their communities. The search for a sense of fulfilment drives people forward. For Muslims and many people in the world today, a successful marriage leading to successful families and right-acting children is a very important part of life. Human beings cannot remain loners; they need friends, spouses and partners to share their thoughts, ideas, experiences, joys and pains. Allah created a partner for the first man so that, as husband and wife, they could live in peace and tranquillity. When they came down to earth they formed the first human family and fulfilled the divine requirement of sowing the seeds of humankind. From these two people in the beginning, there are now over six billion human beings on earth, the diverse human race.

Marriage and family should thus be treated seriously. While marriage is a legal contract between two responsible adults, the family is a part of the bedrock of human society. They cannot be taken casually. To Muslims they are an integral part of their *deen*. No matter in what age or land, they have universal importance.

Building a sound Muslim family is important for most Muslim men and women. Parenting as a civilisational endeavour can only succeed in positive family environments. Muslim parents in the West, given its prevalent socio-cultural and moral conditions, have obviously a most challenging task. The starting point is the understanding of the challenge and then following the footsteps of the early Muslims in the new context. Here comes the primordial importance of good conduct and behaviour in the family. The prophets were sent to teach humanity good conduct and right behaviour. By being the role model in all aspects of family life the last Prophet ﷺ emphasised its importance eloquently,

> "The best of you is the best to his family and I am the best among you to my family". (*Ibn Majah*)

> The most perfect believers are the best in conduct, and the best of you are those who are best to their spouses (*At-Tirmidhi*).

As mentioned, husbands are generally the breadwinners in a family. However, for genuine economic and professional reasons wives in a family may desire to work. They might want to give a helping hand in earning for the family. However, this must not be compromised with the Islamic upbringing and education of children. There should be open and frank discussion and consultation between the spouses for the overall welfare of the family. Children, being at the centre of any planning and action, should be involved as and when necessary, according to their age and maturity. This is important for inculcating in them the sense of responsibility and making them aware of the realities of life.

Families can be life-long schools for human beings. Muslim families are centres of learning if the environment is healthy and positive. The family of the Prophet Muhammad ﷺ, with his measured, lively and meaningful dealings with family members, remains the role model for humanity. There was liveliness without vulgarity, seriousness without tension and competition in *taqwa* without rivalry. It was the reservoir of knowledge and virtue from which the companions ؓ quenched their thirst for knowledge of the conduct of an ideal family.

Life is full of serious and complex issues, but to make it meaningful our body and spirit need space for humour and enjoyment. Both husband and wife should strive to give their partner the joy and pleasure of life. The Messenger of Allah ﷺ used to cut lively, but innocent, jokes with his wives. He ran races with his young wife, Umm al-Mu'minin A'isha. One day he defeated her and said that it was in revenge for his defeat in the previous race! The hadith, "Entertain the hearts in between hours, for if the hearts become tired they become blind" (*Sunan al-Daylami*), is a glowing lesson for us. Lively encounters and a sense of humour bring people closer. The Caliph Umar ﵎ used to advise his people that when men are in their houses with their wives they should behave in a relaxed manner. This insistence on a stress-free life does not mean that a Muslim family loses seriousness when gravity is necessary.

Virtue proliferates in a right-acting family where husband and wife lead a purposeful and happy life. They protect each other and together they protect children in the family. Everyone contributes to the happy atmosphere. Blessed families contribute to a blessed society and ultimately lead toward an ummah of purpose. This is a virtuous cycle. In a sound and responsible family no one can fall through the net. Everyone watches out so that no one becomes lost. Parents and children pray for each other. The maxim, 'the family that prays together stays together', becomes meaningful.

> And the believers, men and women, are protecting friends of one another; they enjoin the right and forbid the wrong, and they establish prayer and they pay the poor-due, and they obey Allah and His Messenger. As for these, Allah will have mercy on them. Verily, Allah is Mighty, Wise. (Qur'an 9:71).

The threat to marriage and family institution comes from the human beings' refusal to accept the supremacy of their Lord in their lives. Their arrogant refusal to become slaves of one Lord makes them slaves of their own whims and desires. Marriage and family do not fit with their egos because they entail rights, responsibility and accountability. They want to enjoy life with unrestrained freedom, no matter whether that harms their long-term future, or their partners and their offspring. This is the day in which we live now. This is the age of the moral maze and spiritual void, the age of proselytising materialism.

However, it is worth noting that human beings are learning from their mistakes and gradually coming back to their senses. The fruits of an irreligious lifestyle is having its toll. The ill effects of cohabitation and rampant extramarital sex are teenage pregnancy, single-parent families, family disintegration, domestic violence and the rise in the number of problem children. All these are eating away at the fabric of community harmony and social stability. It is now costing developed countries economically and socially, leading to gloomy national futures. Human beings are losing their mutual trust, mental peace and the purpose of life. The trend of individualism, consumerism, egoism, uncontrolled promiscuity and sensuality is on the rise. For any society and nation all these can have devastating consequences.

Muslims in the West cannot live in cloud cuckoo land. In a globalised world, particularly in the West, they are gradually becoming vulnerable to this social trend. The shockwaves of these social diseases are having negative effects in their families and communities. Already there are signs of cracks in their families leading to juvenile delinquency, drug abuse, gansterism and crimes, in the cities where Muslims have a significant presence. Already there are signs of confusion among Muslim youth about their identity. Unless addressed with a sense of urgency, things could turn out much more difficult in coming years.

Marriage and family are pillars of a stable society and nation. Our success in this world and the Hereafter depends on how we perform as the emissaries of Allah on earth. Marriage gives us solace and tranquillity of mind and heart. Family gives us an anchor. The love, affection, warmth and emotional attachment created between a man and a woman thrive in marriage and family bonding and are transmitted to our offspring. Together they become the strongest unit, the fortress, of the human race. As such, marriage and family are so vital for human beings to succeed.

72

Bibliography

Abdalhaqq and Aisha Bewley (1999). *The Noble Qur'an: A New rendering of its Meaning in English*, Bookwork, Norwich.

Akhtar, Shabbir (1993). *The Muslim Parents Handbook: What Every Muslim Parent Should Know*, Ta-Ha Publishers, London.

Al-Albani, Muhammad Naasir-ud-deen (1998). *The Etiquettes of Marriage: In the Pure Tradition of the Prophet*, Ihyaa' Minhaaj Al-Sunnah, UK.

Al-Areefee, Yoosuf ibn Abdullah (1996). *Manners of Welcoming the NewBorn Child in Islam*, Maktaba Darus Salaam, UK.

Al-Bukhari, Imam, *Sahih al-Bukhari*, Translated by Dr. Muhammad Muhsin Khan (1997). Darussalam, Riyadh.

Al-Ghazali, M (1989). *Muslim Character*, IIFSO.

Al-Kaysi, Marwan I (1994). *Morals and Manners in Islam: A Guide to Islamic Adab*, The Islamic Foundation, UK.

Altalib, Hisham, (1993). *Training Guide for Islamic Workers*. Herndon, VA: IIIT and IIFSO.

Ali Nadwi, Abul Hasan (1983). *Islam and the World*, IIFSO.

An-Nawawi, Imam, *Riyad-us-Saleheen*, (1998). Islamic Book Service, Delhi.

Asad, Muhammad (1980). *The Message of the Qur'an*, Dar al-Andalus Limited, Gibralter.

Azami, Iqbal A (1990). *Muslim Manners*, UK Islamic Academy, UK.

Bashier, Zakaria (1991). *Makkan Crucible,* The Islamic Foundation, Leicester.

Bashier, Zakaria (1998). *Sunshine at Madinah,* The Islamic Foundation, Leicester.

Beshir, Ekram and Mohamed Rida, (1998). *Meeting the Challenge of Parenting in the West: An Islamic Perspective.* Amanah Publications, USA.

Campion, Mukti J (1993). *The Good Parent Guide,* Element, UK.

Doi, Abdur Rahman I, (1989) *Woman in Shariah,* Ta-Ha, London.

D'Oyen, Fatima M (1996). *The Miracle of Life: A Guide on Islamic Family Life and Sex Education for Young People,* The Islamic Foundation, Leicester.

Eyre, Linda and Richard, (1980). *Teaching Your Children Joy,* Fireside, New York.

Eyre, Linda and Richard, (1993). *Teaching Your Children Values,* Fireside, New York.

Eyre, Linda and Richard, (1994). *Teaching Your Children Responsibility,* Fireside, New York.

Fenwick, Elizabeth and Smith, Dr. Tony, (1994). *Adolescence – The Survival Guide for Parents and Teenagers,* London.

Gaffney, Maureen, et. al, (1991). *Parenting: A Handbook for Parents,* Town House, UK.

Hamid, AbdulWahid (1995). *Companions of the Prophet,* MELS, Leicester.

Haralambos and Holborn Sociology, (1995, 4th Ed). *Sociology: Themes and Perspectives,* Harper Collins, London.

Hammudah Abd al-Ati, (1977). *The Family Structure in Islam,* American Trust Publication.

Hasan, Suhaib (1998). *Raising Children in Islam,* Al-Qur'an Society, London.

Haykal, M. H. (1976). *The Life of Muhammad* ﷺ, American Trust Publication, Indianapolis, USA.

Huda-al-Khattab, (1997). *Bent Rib: A Journey Through Women's Issue in Islam,* Ta-ha Publishers, London.

Imam Ghazzali, (1991). *Ihya Ulum-id-din, Book II*, New Delhi.

Joslin, Karen R, (1994). *The Parent's Problem Solver: Practical Solutions to over 140 Childhood problems*, Vermilion, London.

Klein Mavis and Piatkus Judy, (1991). *Understanding Your Child: An A-Z for Parents*, Piatkus Ltd, London.

Lang, Jeffrey (1997). *Even Angels Ask – A Journey to Islam in America*, Amana Publications, USA.

Lang, Jeffrey (1994). *Struggling to Surrender*, Amana Publications, USA.

Lemu, Aisha and Hereen, Fatima (1978). *Women in Islam*, The Islamic Foundation, Leicester.

Maqsood, Ruqaiyyah Waris (1995). *Living with Teenagers: A Guide for Muslim Parents*, Ta-ha Publishers, London.

Maudoodi, Sayyid, Abul A'la (1982). *Let us be Muslims*, Edited by Khurram Murad, The Islamic Foundation, Leicester.

Maudoodi, Sayyid, Abul A'la (1995). *Towards Understanding Islam*, The Islamic Foundation, Leicester.

Murad, Khurram (2000). *In the Early Hours: Reflections on Spiritual and Self Development*, Revival Publications, the UK.

Muslim, Imam, *Sahih Muslim*, Translated by Abdul Hamid Siddiqi (1990). Ashraf Islamic Publishers, Lahore.

Muslim Students' Association, (1976). *Parents' Manual: A Guide for Muslim Parents Living in North America*, American Trust Publications, USA.

Pickthall, Muhammad Marmaduke, *The Meaning of the Glorious Qur'an: Text and Explanatory Translation*, New American Library.

Rahman, Afzalur (1986). *Role of Muslim Woman in Society*, Seerah Foundation, London.

Sabiq, As-Sayyid (1404AH). *Fiqh-us-Sunnah*, Dar El Fateh for Arab Information, Plainfield, Indiana.

Sarwar, G (1996). *Sex Education: The Muslim Perspective*, The Muslim Educational Trust, London.

At-Tirmidhi, Imam, *Shama'il Tirmidhi* (2001). Darul Ishaat, Karachi.

Wali Muhammad, Matina (1994). *Stories: Good and True for Children* (translated), Ta-Ha Publishers, London.

Yusuf Ali, Abdullah (1997) *The Holy Qur'an,* Islamic Book Service, Delhi.

Glossary of Islamic Terms

Adab	Good manners, etiquette, custom. In Islam it has ethical and social implications. It includes the meaning of civility, courtesy and refinement.
Adhan	Call to prayer uttered loudly summoning Muslims to pray together behind the imam in the mosque.
'Adl	Justice, fairness, equilibrium and equity. A fundamental value governing social behaviour, dealings and the legal framework.
Allah	Creator and Sustainer of all. This Arabic word is unique. It has no feminine and no plural. No other word, in any language, carries the meaning of 'Allah'.
Ahl al-Kitab	People of the Book, i.e. those people who received an authentic revelation before Islam, meaning the Jews and Christians. The judgement has been extended to some degree to other religions. People of the Book may live under the governance of Islam by their own revelations and laws, under certain conditions.
Akhirah	Hereafter. The Day of Judgement and the life after death. One of the articles of faith in Islam.
ﷺ 'alaihi's-s-salam	May Allah's peace be upon him.
Amanah	Trust. Something given to someone for safekeeping.

	The human being undertook The Trust offered by Allah, and if true to that trust he is said to have *iman*.
Amir	Leader, lit.: 'commander'. A term applied both to the Caliph and to subsidiary and other leaders in general.
Ansar	Lit.: helpers. In specific meaning, companions of Prophet Muhammad ﷺ in Madinah who helped the Prophet ﷺ and his companions when they migrated from Makkah to Madinah.
'Aqiqah	Sacrifice of an animal and feeding people from its meat out of joy and gratitude at the birth of a baby.
'Asabiyyah	Tribal loyalty and the whole complex of relationships to be found in natural peoples because of their kin structures. Where people put it and the needs of their group or clan ahead of the deen of Allah and the needs of the whole community it becomes a blameworthy concept.
As-salamu 'alaikum	The Islamic greeting, 'Peace be upon you'.
Awqaf (sing. Waqf)	A trusteeship. Endowment. An inalienable property whose ownership is returned to Allah and whose use is dedicated to some purpose usually of a charitable nature. Most of the social welfare of the Muslims was taken care of by means of *awqaf*, and in the nineteenth century as much as two-thirds of Ottoman land and property was in the form of such charitable endowments.
Ayat (sing. ayah)	Verses of the Qur'an. It literally means a sign or an indication, and also means a miracle.
Caliph/Khalifah	The leader of the Muslim ummah.
Da'wah	Invitation, call. Refers to the duty of Muslims to invite others to submission to Allah and the natural path of Islam.
Deen	The life-transaction. More than 'religion' since it encompasses all aspects of life including buying and selling, and the governance of the Muslims.

Du'a	Supplication to Allah.
Dunya	The present world. It stems from a root which means *lower* or *nearer.*
'Eid	Celebration. Eid al-Fitr is the celebration upon conclusion of the month of fasting and 'Eid al-Adha is the celebration of sacrifice upon conclusion of the Hajj.
Fajr	Dawn. The very first light at the end of the night.
Fiqh	Islamic jurisprudence, from a verb which means 'to understand'.
Fitrah	Nature, natural condition of the human being.
Hadith (pl. Ahadith)	Literally, an account. Accounts of the sayings, deeds and tacit approvals of the Messenger of Allah ﷺ.
Hadith Qudsi	Sayings of Prophet Muhammad ﷺ in which he quotes the words of Allah, when he mentioned 'Allah has said ...'. It is distinct from the Qur'an which is the words of Allah sent by the medium of the angel Jibril ﷺ.
Hafidh (pl. Huffadh)	A Muslim who memorises the whole Qur'an by heart. Among Muslim scholars it is furthermore taken to refer to someone who having memorised the Qur'an has also committed to memory substantial numbers of ahadith.
Hajj	Pilgrimage. Once in a lifetime journey of a physically and economically capable adult Muslim to Makkah. Elements in it stem from the time of Adam ﷺ, and from the sacrifice of the prophet Ibrahim ﷺ.
Halal	Permissible. Lawful. Anything permitted by Islamic Shari'ah.
Haram	Unlawful. Anything prohibited by the Shari'ah.
Hayah	Modesty, shame.
Hijab	Modest dress worn by a Muslim woman, and in particular that which covers her hair.

Hilf al-Fudhul	A welfare organisation during the youth and pre-prophetic period of the life of the Prophet Muhammad ﷺ to serve people in need, and to see that justice was done in the society.
'Ibadah	Worship, obedience to Allah.
Iblis	He was a member of the unseen Jinn, who fell from Allah's grace and became cursed because of his refusal to submit to Adam, and because of his disobedience and arrogance. From him have come many *shayatin* (pl. of *shaytan*), from among both the Jinn and mankind.
Ijtihad	Exertion of independent judgement in light of Islamic guidance and authentic knowledge. It is the disciplined use of reasoning to draw a necessary conclusion in accordance with both the law and the spirit of Islam. It may only be exercised by a competent exponent of Fiqh whose excellence is universally acknowledged by other scholars and who, some hold, is authorised by the Caliph or a Sultan to do so.
'Ilm	Knowledge. In Islam this includes empirical as well as legal knowledge of the Shari'ah and transcendental knowledge, and in fact means unqualified knowledge.
Imam	Today it means a person who leads congregational prayers. Also a reputable scholar but, in its original meaning, the leader of the Muslim community.
Iman	Belief in and affirmation of the articles of iman enunciated in the Qur'an and the Sunnah: i.e. belief in Allah, His Messengers, His Books, His angels, the Last Day and that the Decree of good and evil is from Him. Iman, which can increase or decrease, is the doorway to Islam.
Islam	Literally to submit and to offer peace. Life-transaction (see Deen) of submission to the will of Allah, expounded by all the prophets.

Istikharah	Special prayer intended to ask for an indication or guidance from Allah when taking a difficult decision as to which choice is likely to be of benefit.
Jahiliyyah	Ignorance (of divine guidance). Refers to the later part of the period between prophet 'Isa (Jesus) 🕮 and the Messenger of Allah 🕮 when people forgot the teachings of the prophets.
Jihad	Literally, to struggle, to make effort. Striving to create a just society which worships Allah. It also means armed struggle. It must be for the sake of Allah. It also includes one's continuous effort to shun one's selfish whims, desires and appetites.
Ka'bah	Literally, cube. The cube-shaped building in Makkah built by the prophet Ibrahim 🕮 and his son Isma'il 🕮, as the first house for the worship of Allah. Said to have been originally built at the time of Adam 🕮. The direction all Muslims face when praying, and the locus to which they gravitate when performing the 'Umrah or Hajj.
Kalimah	Literally, word, and sometimes intending the phrase, "There is no god but Allah, Muhammad is Allah's Messenger", the conscious uttering of which makes someone a Muslim.
Khidmah	Service, working for the welfare of human beings.
Khul'	The process through which a Muslim woman obtains a divorce from her husband through an Islamic court. If a Muslim woman finds that she is simply incompatible with her husband, she may offer to return some or all of her dowry or in some other manner to compensate him, and thus obtain a divorce.
Madrasah	School, but traditionally a school for study of the deen.
Mahr	Dower, a compulsory due (cash or kind) to a bride from the groom according to the groom's financial ability.

Mahram	Blood relation with whom marriage is forbidden. *Ghair Mahram* is someone who does not fall into the category of Mahram.
Masnun	From the Sunnah. There are specific *Masnun Du'a* for specific occasions.

Muhajir (pl. Muhajirun) Literally, an emigrant. The early Muslims who migrated to Madinah from Makkah with the Prophet ﷺ in order to be able to practise the deen without fear, and to escape from persecution.

Mujahid	Related to the word Jihad. One who strives for the cause of Allah.
Murabbi	One who undertakes another's upbringing, whether as a parent or as teacher or instructor in later life.
Muslim	A believer who willingly submits to Allah alone and practises Islam.
Nafsaniat	Whims and desires of the *nafs*–self that lead a human being toward wrongdoing. Among the most obstinate and dangerous of such traits are the subtle desires of a person to be recognised and respected in the community.
Nasheed	Islamic song, meaningful and instructional in content and comprising *dhikr*-remembrance of Allah and asking blessings on the Messenger of Allah ﷺ.
Nifaq	Hypocrisy, two-facedness and double standards which are deplorable in Islam. Originally it signified in its major form someone who insincerely accepted Islam. According to a hadith, the signs of Nifaq are – lying, breaking promises, and abuse or misuse of trust.
Nikah	Marriage according to a simple Islamic contract.
Qist	Similar to 'Adl. Justice, fairness, equilibrium and equity. A fundamental value governing social behaviour, dealings and legal framework.
Qur'an	The final Book and revelation from Allah to hu-

mankind, revealed to the Prophet Muhammad ﷺ over a span of 23 years.

❧ Radi'Allahu 'anhu   (Fem. Radi'Allahu 'anha, pl. ❧ Radi'Allahu 'anhum). May Allah be pleased with him (her).

❧ Radi'Allahu 'anhum. May Allah be pleased with them.

Rahmah	Mercy.
Ramadan	The 9th month of the Islamic calendar during which Muslims fast from dawn to sunset.
Risalah	The Message, the revelation and the shari'ah itself, and the concept that Allah sent prophets to human beings to guide them. One of the articles of faith in Islam.
Ruh	Spirit.
Ruku'	Bowing. The specific physical posture during the daily prayers.
Sabr	Steadfastness. The word has a wider and more positive meaning in Islam than simple patient endurance of suffering.
Sahabah	Companions of the Prophet Muhammad ﷺ during his lifetime. There are many hadith that indicate they were the best of all generations of humanity.
Sahih	Literally 'sound'. A hadith whose chain of narrators are each authentic in their beliefs, characters, scholarship and memories and who each have received it directly from the previous such narrator in the chain of transmission which connects directly back to the Messenger of Allah ﷺ. Higher than it in status is the *Mutawatir* hadith which is transmitted by so many different chains of narration that there can be no possible doubt about its authenticity.
Sajdah	Prostration. The specific physical posture during the daily prayers.
Sakinah	Tranquillity of mind that comes due to the blessings of Allah

Sayyiduna	Our master. A term of respect.
Sirah	The biography of the Messenger of Allah ﷺ from authentic sources.
Shari'ah	Derived from a work meaning 'a road' particularly one leading to water in the desert. Used to mean Islam's legal system and the rules by which Muslims abide.
Shahadah	Literally, witnessing. Declaration of the acceptance of Islam.
Sunnah	pl. Sunan. Literally, a custom or practice. The body of practices of the Prophet Muhammad ﷺ. It also includes the practice established by the rightly guided first four Caliphs. It is sometimes mistakenly assumed to be synonymous with hadith.
Surah	Chapter of the Qur'an. There are 114 Surah, some of which are very long and others short.
Taharah	Cleanliness that entails bodily and ritual purity.
Tajdid	Revival, enlivening.
Talaq	Divorce initiated by men. There are Shari'ah requirements for it.
Taqwa	Fear or consciousness of Allah that leads to abandonment of wrong action and embodiment of right action. It is both an inner feeling of a human being towards the Creator and the effects of that upon his actions.
Tarbiyah	Nurturing, training. Physical, moral, intellectual and spiritual development. The modern Arabic term for education. The person who undertakes such instruction is Murabbi.
Tawakkul	Reliance on Allah. It gives mental tranquillity.
Tawhid	The concept of the absolute Oneness of Allah. The fundamental article of faith in Islam.
Tazkiyah	Purification. Growth.

'Ulama (sing. 'Alim)   People of knowledge. The term has wrongly become confined to religious scholars.

Ummah   Community of believers worldwide, irrespective of race, colour, language or geographical boundary. The universal body of Muslims as a single community, properly when living by the Shari'ah and living under the governance of Islamic rulers.

Umm al-Mu'minin Mother of the believers (a name for each of the Prophet Muhammad's wives)

'Umrah   Lesser pilgrimage to Makkah with specific rites.

Zakah   The compulsory yearly due payable by a wealthy Muslim, as a part of his obligation, mainly for the benefit of the poor and the needy. Its amount is 2.5% on his cash and on the proceeds of business, 10% or 20% of crops, and specific proportions of cattle, the cash to be paid in gold and silver, and the other categories to be paid in kind to the authorised zakat collectors of an Amir who may, if necessary, take it by force. This pillar is wrongly thought to be an act of personal charity left to the conscious of the individual Muslim.

The
Muslim
Woman's
Hand Book

HUDA KHATTAB

The Noble Woman

Aliya Butt

The Life of
Muhammad
صلى الله عليه وسلم
his life based on the earliest sources

Tahia Al-Ismail

Ta-Ha Publishers Ltd.
1, Wynne Road, London, SW9 OBD.